"Angela has a gift for clearly articulating deep, complicated emotions in a way that few writers can. I admire both her gut-level honesty and her thorough reflection. Her poignant storytelling gives readers permission to embrace the messiness of life and reinvigorates our hope in God's presence through it all."

— Linda Livingstone
president of Baylor University

"Angela Gorrell's moving personal experiences and stories in *The Gravity of Joy* arise amidst the ordinary, exceptional, and anguishing realities of being human. She is a vulnerable and honest guide, who knows her own and others' tear-stained cheeks, as she and others receive joy with wonder, not triumph; with humility, not presumption; with presence, not power. This book is a witness to hope that can and does save lives."

— Mark Labberton
president of Fuller Theological Seminary

"Angela Gorrell was part of a Yale Divinity School project on 'a theology of joy' when three members of her family died within four weeks, all in tragic situations. Drowning in an ocean of sorrow, she wondered if joy could keep her afloat. This remarkable book is her honest, vulnerable, and healing answer to that question. There is no spiritual cheerleading here, no cheap grace. Instead, there is the hard-won knowledge that, while we cannot make joy, we can open ourselves to the God who suffers with us, offering us witness and 'withness.' The night is long, but if we keep on opening and offering ourselves through our tears, joy will come in the morning."

— Parker J. Palmer
author of *On the Brink of Everything, A Hidden Wholeness,*
and *Let Your Life Speak*

"What is the true life? That is the big question that animates this book. Angela Gorrell teaches us that in a well-lived life emotions are felt authentically, choices are embraced meaningfully, and self-transcending connections are forged broadly. These pages crackle with raw honesty, deep wisdom, profound realizations, and potent reminders that ultimately goodness can be found amidst the rancor of daily life. The author's insights contained within are not ivory tower speculations, either. They were formed and forged through the crucible of living. Suffering is inevitable and inescapable but does not have to have the final say in our lives. Joy is a gift and 'will always find us,' writes Gorrell. You will find joy in these pages—may we all be grateful for this deeply moving gift she has given us."

— Robert Emmons
author of *The Psychology of Ultimate Concerns*
and *The Little Book of Gratitude*

"*The Gravity of Joy* is a story of hope in hard times. Angela Gorrell artfully tells her story of faith, pain, and joy. She weaves it with the stories of others—family, women she met in prison Bible study, students, travelers she met on her journey. And she shares a truth that perhaps is discovered only by those who have faced love and loss—especially those society has used and abused, denied dignity to in life and death: that joy comes in the mourning. I encourage all who hunger for justice, peace, acceptance, and comfort to read this book. In its pages you will find beautiful prose and hope that even in the darkest of spaces, places, and times—through addiction, suicide, sudden death, prison, abuse, and despair—love reigns, truth reigns, joy reigns."

— Liz Theoharis
co-chair of the Poor People's Campaign:
A Call for National Revival

"*The Gravity of Joy* is a unique exercise in vulnerable theology. Weaving memoir and journalism, theology and testimony, Gorrell invites us into the unthinkable to discover the possibility of a joy that surpasses understanding. Written with eyes wide open, this book is a reminder that the cracks in a broken heart can be openings for grace."

— James K. A. Smith
author of *You Are What You Love*
and *On the Road with Saint Augustine*

"In *The Gravity of Joy* Angela Gorrell courageously narrates her personal experience of clawing her way through the valley of the shadow of death and despair, yearning for hope yet questioning whether joy can possibly exist in a world where suicide and opioid addiction steal lives away. When she begins to lead a Bible study with incarcerated women, she finds unexpected balm for her own despair, leading her to affirm: 'By grappling with suffering we actually come to a clearer understanding of joy. . . . God's primary response to suffering is *withness* and *witness*—the visible manifestation of God's presence in the midst of suffering.'"

— Joyce Ann Mercer
Horace Bushnell Professor of Christian Nurture
at Yale Divinity School

The Gravity of Joy

A Story of Being Lost and Found

Angela Williams Gorrell

WILLIAM B. EERDMANS PUBLISHING COMPANY

GRAND RAPIDS, MICHIGAN

Wm. B. Eerdmans Publishing Co.
4035 Park East Court SE, Grand Rapids, Michigan 49546
www.eerdmans.com

Published 2021
Printed in the United States of America

27 26 25 24 23 22 21   1 2 3 4 5 6 7

ISBN 978-0-8028-7794-9

Library of Congress Cataloging-in-Publication Data

Names: Gorrell, Angela, 1982– author.
Title: The gravity of joy : a story of being lost and found / Angela
    Williams Gorrell.
Description: Grand Rapids, Michigan : William B. Eerdmans
    Publishing Company, [2021] | Includes bibliographical refer-
    ences. | Summary: "An extended reflection on finding authentic
    Christian joy in the midst of suffering and despair, especially
    the twenty-first-century epidemics of suicide and addiction"—
    Provided by publisher.
Identifiers: LCCN 2020040447 | ISBN 9780802877949
Subjects: LCSH: Joy—Religious aspects—Christianity. | Suffering—
    Religious aspects—Christianity. | Despair—Religious aspects—
    Christianity. | Suicide—Religious aspects—Christianity. |
    Addicts—Religious life
Classification: LCC BV4647.J68 G67 2021 | DDC 248.8/6—dc23
LC record available at https://lccn.loc.gov/2020040447

For Dustin, Mason, and Dad,
we miss you terribly.
Life is not the same without you.

For the women in the prison Bible study group,
may the joy you brought me be yours, too.

Contents

Foreword

In this book you'll read stories of Angela Williams Gorrell's pain and joy during the three years she worked for the Yale Center for Faith & Culture and co-taught the Life Worth Living course at Yale University. You will learn of the pain of her own loss and the pain she bore on behalf of others, as well as of the joy that came to her and the joy that she elicited in others. You will learn much about the impact of people on her. But what you won't get from the book, and what you need to know while reading it, is the magnitude of the impact she's had on people around her, most notably her students.

I could never do what Angela does. I could never be the kind of teacher she is. She has chosen to close this book by mentioning her final lecture to the Life Worth Living class, delivered at the end of her time at Yale. She sums up what she told students she hoped they would take with them from her teaching. But she doesn't tell what happened immediately after that lecture, how her students, full of joy, gathered around her. To say that she was a "star" to them would be to say too little and, perhaps, to wrongly place emphasis on her "success" as a teacher. Instead, it seemed that she became a kind of flesh-and-blood "angel" to them, an unusual messenger, struggling with pain and, in openness about the struggle, bearing witness to life's new possibilities. As one of the co-teachers of the course, I was in the room when she gave that lecture. I had taught Life Worth Living four times prior to that. In fact, together with Ryan McAnnally-Linz, I had originally designed the course. It's a popular class, and I have always sensed students' appreciation for and excitement about it. But they never surrounded me on the last day of class as they surrounded Angela, moved by affection for her and beckoned by the world that she opened up for them. Much of their devotion to her had to do with how she herself dealt with the pain she experienced and with the path to joy she found in it.

Like that class, for Angela this book is not about Angela, though stories of her experiences figure very prominently in it. It is about the great power of that rather ephemeral but irresistible emotion called joy, an emotion that we cannot manufacture but that we can prepare for and open ourselves toward. It is an emotion deeply and uniquely ours and yet, the wider the circle of those with whom we share in it, the richer and deeper it becomes for us. It is an emotion bound up with the goods of this world, but which the world can neither strictly give nor fully take away. It is an emotion that seeks its own eternity and therefore the eternity of all the goods to which it is a fitting response. In writing this book, Angela seeks to address a culture "obsessed with synthetic happiness and riddled with pain," a culture, in fact, in which pain, often bereft of other resources, aches for synthetic happiness and in which synthetic happiness, in turn, demands payment for its services in the currency of life-destroying addiction and despair. To break the cycle, Angela writes an ode to the kind of joy that was, as the Gospel of Luke attests, at the heart of the message of Jesus Christ. That joy, Christ's joy, is "an incredibly powerful counteragent to despair—and even a companion during suffering." In a way—a difficult, challenging way—each of the stories of addiction, despair, depression, and death Angela here tells is an invitation to that kind of joy.

MIROSLAV VOLF
Henry B. Wright Professor of Theology, Yale Divinity School
Founder and Director, Yale Center for Faith and Culture

A Note about How
This Book Came to Be

Throughout this book, I tell my story.

I do this to the best of my ability, recognizing that memory can be faulty. My aim was to focus on how events that I witnessed affected me personally (how I perceived what happened and to what effect). Along the way, I implicated others who were involved in my story. In order to try and tell my story as truthfully as possible, I invited everyone that I could, whose stories are implicated alongside mine, to read the book and to help me make sure the stories are truthful. I was unable to ask the women in the prison Bible study to read this book, but I asked several Bible study team members to read it for accuracy. I changed the names of the Bible study coleaders and the names and physical descriptions of the women in prison as well as the name of anyone else who asked me to do so, in order to conceal particular people's identities as much as possible.

Additionally, this book utilizes journalism. My graduate assistant, Joy Moton, has a bachelor's degree in journalism. She helped me to research other people who had also been affected by suicide and opioid addiction. She set up journalistic interviews with them and helped me create questions that we used during the interviews. I also set up two phone calls with two people who are doing important work related to responding to addiction—Trevor at the front lines of the opioid crisis and Nina, who runs Council Circle groups. I reported people's reflections from these interviews as accurately as possible. Each person who told their story to us in this format has confirmed that I represented their interview accurately.

This book works to integrate research, Christian theology, and critical and theological reflection on lived experience in order to consider joy as a counteragent to America's crisis of despair. My process was neither linear nor calculated. I began writing my story and interwove research on joy, suicide, and addiction as I wrote. This book reflects my training as a practical theologian. It demonstrates cycles of action and reflection, with a specific concern for understanding despair and joy from the perspective of multiple disciplines while trying to account for these things in a coherent, comprehensive way that takes seriously people's lives—mine and others.

This book shares, together with my story, findings about joy from the Theology of Joy and the Good Life project, a grant managed by Miroslav Volf and his team at the Yale Center for Faith and Culture (YCFC, of which I was formerly a part) and generously funded by the John Templeton Foundation (JTF). My lived experience and the project participants' research on joy are in dialogue throughout the book. My lived experience caused me to read participants' research on joy in a particular light, and participants' research helped me to understand joy as experienced in my life. In this way, throughout the book, there is a dialogical interplay between joy research and lived experience.

Before writing this book, as part of my job at YCFC, I read multiple books and articles on joy to try to gain an understanding of joy research from several disciplines. At times this scholarship informs the content of this book, indicated by notes. Before and while writing this book, my work at YCFC also involved reading papers and articles by the joy project's scholars and participating in joy research consultations, meetings, and informal conversations. These three years of joy conversation are "written on my heart," so to speak, and they inform this book. I have noted every participant in the joy project who informed this book in a particular and obvious way.

As I wrote this book, I reread many papers and articles and drew on participants' ideas and research for my account of joy.

The people who reflected on joy during the project were not necessarily trying to find consensus on the topic; rather, each participant brought their own convictions and research to conversations, meetings, lectures, and papers for research consultations. However, I have utilized various participants' reflections as a form of literary review of joy, and at times I have chosen to reflect on joy from various people's perspectives in an integrated way even though the people I cite may not agree with one another.

Prologue

America's crisis of despair crashed into my life while I was getting paid to think about joy.

In early 2016, I was hired at the Yale Center for Faith and Culture to work on the Theology of Joy and the Good Life project. I accepted the job to research joy and visions of the good life with great enthusiasm. It's important work. Many of us don't sense joy. We don't know how to become open to it, how to seek it, or how to share our longing for it. And often, even when it comes, we do not feel free to express it.

Positive emotions like joy can be viewed as shallow or trivial. Perhaps we believe expressing joy, especially in a world with so much pain and loss, is disrespectful, naive, and privileged. When we think about joy like this, we overlook its capacity to be an incredibly powerful counteragent to despair—and even a companion during suffering.

Less than a year after I was hired to think about joy, three of my family members unexpectedly died within four weeks.

These weeks of hell turned America's dramatic rise in suicide into something personal. I had known people who had suicidal thoughts, but before December 2016 I had never known someone who died by suicide. The suicide of my cousin's husband changed that.

A month later, my dad died after years of using prescription opioids. Chronic pain had changed him from a fun, loving, passionate person into someone holed up in a bedroom addicted to pills, and he slipped away from us. Another national news topic—America's opioid crisis—became intensely personal and deeply painful.

In between *those* two funerals, my nephew died unexpectedly at twenty-two of sudden cardiac arrest. Mason's death was not tied to anything in news headlines, yet it represents the timeless story of senseless death too soon. And more pain and grief, suffering that feels pointless.

My vocation was supposed to be joy, and I was speaking at funerals.

It was not until a few weeks after Dad's funeral that I began to realize the psychological, physical, emotional, and spiritual toll of experiencing three traumatizing deaths in such a short time.

In the fog of grief, everything in my life turned gray and I struggled to get out of bed most days. It seemed as if I was losing my grip on the faith I had known so clearly all my life. Studying joy was still my job, but reading about it, thinking about it, and talking about it didn't mean I recognized it or felt it.

Then, in what can only be ascribed to an act of grace, I became a part of a team leading a Bible study at a women's prison. This experience changed my life. Many of these women had also wrestled with addiction and thoughts of suicide. They had suffered and were still suffering, and yet they showed a tremendous capacity for joy. Around the same time, I heard my friend, theologian Willie James Jennings, talk about "making pain productive, without justifying or glorifying suffering." He described the work of joy in the midst of pain.

I wondered: Would the illuminations scholars shared with us about joy during the joy project stand the tests of my suffering and the profound suffering of others? What is joy in the face of suicide, addiction, and sudden loss? Can it be found?

I realized that if research on joy could not speak to the despair present in America today—especially that of addiction and suicide—then it *was* too shallow.

What I learned wasn't simple or easy, because joy isn't simple and it's not always easy—at least not in those times when we feel its need most acutely. It turns out that joy has grit. It isn't fluffy or ephemeral. Joy is what we feel deep in our bones when we realize and feel connected to what is good, beautiful, meaningful.

And joy unites us to one another.

Joy doesn't obliterate grief. Grief doesn't just vanish because joy comes. Instead, joy has a mysterious capacity to be felt alongside sorrow and even—sometimes most especially—in the midst of suffering.

This book describes connections between suicidal thinking, addiction, and despair, and it prescribes joy as the counteragent to despair.

I write as a practical theologian and pastor who has experienced the impacts of suicide and addiction, and who has been able to find joy—or it found me (more on this later).

The stories in this book are meant to help you to long for joy and expect it, to recognize it and give in to it. They are meant to help you understand why joy can be felt in the midst of sorrow and suffering. I am going to tell my story with the hope and prayer that you will be encouraged and strengthened to tell yours.

Please also allow this book to guide your community in creating space for its members to tell their stories. You can read this book by yourself, of course, but I hope you have the chance to read it along with other people.

Beyond this, I pray this book can be a catalyst to bring people together to address two major health crises of our time: suicide and opioid addiction and overdose. The diagnosis of despair—with its main elicitors: pain, shame, loneliness, and feelings of worthlessness—is something that requires a groundswell of people to confront and heal, with God's help.

The more I have shared my grief and related experiences openly, the more I've discovered other people who have lived or are living with similar loss, pain, fear, or anger. And I've seen over and over a similar yearning for joy. Learning to tell our stories honestly allows us to grieve and find helpful relief from pain, connects us with other people, and provides perspective and healing. And those things make room for joy.

But before we can fully believe joy is the counteragent to despair that it is, most of us have to first get to a point like I did, like the women I met in prison did, like so many people grieving and struggling with suicidal thoughts and addiction do—to the point of *yearning for joy.*

To get there, we first need to walk together through the shadows.

1

Sheer Silence

You, God, who live next door—
If at times, through the long night,
    I trouble you
with my urgent knocking—
this is why: I hear you breathe so seldom.
I know you're all alone in that room.
If you should be thirsty, there's no one
to get you a glass of water.
I wait listening, always. Just give me
    a sign!
I'm right here.
As it happens, the wall between us
is very thin. Why couldn't a cry from one
    of us
break it down? It would crumble easily,
it would barely make a sound.

        —From Rainer Maria Rilke's
           Book of Hours:
           Love Poems to God

The *New York Times* headline reads, "The Insatiable and Unknowable Anthony Bourdain." And reporter Frank Bruni writes: "Anthony Bourdain devoured the world. That's not hyperbole. It's not even metaphor. There was no place that he wasn't curious to explore, no food that he wasn't determined to try, no cap on his hunger and no ceiling, or so it always seemed, on his joy."

Anthony Bourdain spent decades in kitchens, largely unknown. He began working in Cape Cod as a dishwasher in a restaurant when he was a teenager. Bourdain eventually went to culinary school and worked as a line cook, sous-chef, and restaurant manager for several years, many of which he spent addicted to heroin, as he often openly discussed.

It was not until his forties, after writing an article for *The New Yorker*, that audiences worldwide learned who he was. His article turned into a best-selling book, *Kitchen Confidential*, and scored him international acclaim; it was translated into twelve languages. Subsequently he became an executive chef. Bourdain authored several more books, owned multiple restaurants, and worked on numerous TV shows. He even played himself in the Oscar-nominated film *The Big Short*.

Bruni explains: "Bourdain's image, as conveyed through his epicurean odysseys, combined flavors of daring, irreverence and supreme confidence. He was appetite incarnate. He was wanderlust with a lavishly stamped passport and an impish, irresistible grin."

On his celebrated show "Parts Unknown," where he ate in all types of places across the globe, Bourdain asked people questions about their happiness, culture, and community. He is often described as an incredible storyteller. Bourdain wanted to help people to encounter others whom they might fear and to see them not as "other" but as an extension of their own humanity.

Bourdain was seemingly doing what he loved—exploring the world, getting to know other cultures, and constantly drinking fantastic beverages and eating delicious food. To most onlookers it would appear that Anthony Bourdain was living the good life.

Yet on June 8, 2018, the world woke up to the news that during the middle of filming a new season of his famous TV show, Bourdain had died by suicide.

There were no illegal substances in his body.

Bourdain's life and death are testaments to the fact that someone can appear to be living the good life and yet not believe their life is worth living. Bruni reflects, "In his writing and especially on his TV shows . . . he exhorted the rest of us to follow his lead and open our eyes and our guts to the wondrous smorgasbord of life. He insisted that we savor every last morsel of it. It turns out that he himself could not."

The persistent question is, "Why?" The question of *why* always follows suicide.

I know.

———

The last time I saw Dustin was on an extended family beach trip.

We all stayed in a massive, rented beach house right near the sand. It was about as perfect as a trip could be with tons of little kids and adults who have not always played nice staying together under one roof. We did what every family does on vacation at the beach—we played in the sunshine, in the ocean, and in the large house; we shared meals and took afternoon naps.

One night a bunch of us went to Joe's Crab Shack and wore plastic bibs, sang, and danced with the kids under the stars to pop music.

During the trip, we took a family photo. When it was time to take the photo we all dressed in similar colors, something a few family members (some of the moms in the group) insisted on. As corny as it was, the rest of us knew it would make the photo better.

My husband, Paul, set up the camera. He put a timer on it and had all of us huddle together.

Half of the adults had kids on their laps. We were all trying to take this as seriously as possible, but naturally it was difficult since our clothes were matching and we were so close to one another, trying to produce smiles on demand.

Paul clicked the camera to start the timer. We all got even closer together and tried not to laugh.

As Paul ran from the camera to join us in the photo before the timer ended, he slipped on a toy, went flying through the air, and landed on the ground.

We all lost it.

We could not contain ourselves as we laughed until many of us had tears running down our cheeks. It took several minutes to collect ourselves and try again.

The weekend was full of those exceptional moments among family members, those times when we put aside our differences and, well, put aside everything actually—work, politics, problems, stress, and all the other things that often dominate our thoughts. They are times when, for just a few days, we do nothing else but be present to one another.

At the end of our time together at the beach, we gave each other big hugs and said we looked forward to gathering together again at Christmas.

I did not know that hugging Dustin in the driveway of the rented beach house would be the last time that I would see him alive.

It took me approximately nine months of crying weekly and seven months of therapy to be able to write the following paragraphs. Even still, as I write these words my heart is beating fast. The text, the call, the phone hitting the pavement—it is all still so disturbing.

It was a Sunday, exactly one week before Christmas.

I woke up and had my usual cup of coffee. It was a leisurely, relaxed morning. While getting ready for church I talked with Mom on the phone about the upcoming Christmas festivities.

The extended family was going to get together at my younger sister Jenna's house on Friday night, the night before Christmas Eve. We were going to have a potluck, eat yummy treats, exchange gifts, and play games. I was excited to see everyone and laugh together again as we had at the beach house just months before.

After the church's Sunday morning service, I headed with Paul and the youth group he led to eat lunch and then sing Christmas carols at two health care centers in our community.

I left my cell phone on the floorboard of our car before heading to the festivities.

We walked through hallways caroling and then to each of the facilities' common areas to sing some more. In the common areas the residents at the health care centers and some staff members joined us in singing. It was a beautiful couple of hours of cheerful songs among multiple generations.

Afterward, the youths and their leaders went back to our church to play reindeer games, eat cookies, and drink Paul's homemade hot chocolate in the church basement.

After we cleaned up, I walked out to our car in the parking lot. Paul was finishing some other tasks. I opened the passenger door and grabbed my cell phone from the floorboard of the car.

I was stunned to discover that I had seven missed calls from Mom and a text from her.

The text read, "Dustin killed himself."

No sentence has devastated me the way this one did. Hearing that a loved one has died by suicide is a swift punch in the gut. It's nauseating. It's what nightmares are made of.

Tears streamed down my face like water rushing over a tub filled to the brim. Before thinking, I called Mom back. I remember screaming "No!" over and over again, crying and demanding she tell me it wasn't true.

The urge to deny that suicide has happened is immediate and seemingly uncontrollable. No one wants to believe that someone they love would hurt themselves to the point of death.

I was wandering through the parking lot as I listened to her tell me that it was true. She was still crying when she answered the phone, though she had known for a few hours.

Suddenly, I dropped the phone on the pavement of the church parking lot and wailed.

The world stopped, and it seemed everyone and everything was silenced.

Even God.

Paul walked out of the church to the parking lot and found me in the most distraught and panicked state he'd ever seen. He was immediately heartbroken too. But honestly, those minutes are so blurry I cannot recall exactly what he said or did.

I do remember that we both knew immediately that we needed to go to Kentucky as soon as possible. We lived in Connecticut, so we knew we would need to pack and drive there early the next morning. We were unsure how long we would stay, so driving seemed like the best option.

Paul called the pastor of the church.

We saw her car in her driveway; she lived in the church parsonage. We thought we would be polite and just call to tell her what happened and ask if Paul could go to Kentucky. We sat in our car in the church parking lot while he made the call and explained to her what had happened. I was crying in the seat next to him, and I cannot imagine that she could not hear my sobs.

I cried for the next week, nearly every hour.

Paul told the pastor that we had just finished leading the youth group Christmas activities; he told her we were still next door and had just found out that a family member had taken his own life.

The pastor said he could go to Kentucky. But she did not come to find us in the parking lot. She did not pray for him over the phone.

This foreshadowed what was to come. It was the beginning of months of attending this church and being met with silence on the part of the church's congregants about what we had faced.

Their silence further deepened the silence of God.

Unfortunately, people don't know what to do or say after suicide and often believe they shouldn't bring it up, so they say nothing, imagining their silence is somehow a help.

But after Dustin's suicide I preferred lots of noise, desperate to remember that I was not alone in suicide's aftermath. So I hoped that people would call, write, text, drop off a basket at the door— find some way to acknowledge the pain.

There were too many days, especially Sunday mornings, when it felt like I was suffocating, and everyone knew, but no one cared.

Nine months earlier, I had accepted a job at Yale to work on the Theology of Joy and the Good Life project.

After being offered the job and saying yes, I took a deep breath and my shoulders loosened. I had roughly fourteen dollars in my bank account. For the first time in over a year, I was not feeling the effects of near paralyzing anxiety.

It seemed as if everything was going to be all right.

The research team I joined was tasked with developing a network of scholars and practitioners with various areas of expertise to investigate joy and visions of flourishing life from diverse perspectives. It was incredible to imagine being a part of such a project. As part of our work, we were also tasked with writing about these topics.

We would also be teaching a course for Yale College students called Life Worth Living.

Leaving Los Angeles was very difficult. It was my home in every sense of the word. I had lived there for thirteen years. Though I did not want to move, I felt like this was the beginning of a new season. I had been stressed out for five years pursuing a PhD and working several part-time jobs.

Now I was going to learn about joy while living the respected, comfortable life of an Ivy League scholar.

I had no way of knowing then that the grief of moving was just the beginning of what was to be the most painful years of my life.

I walked into the basement of Yale's Whitney Humanities Center. I was about forty-five minutes early to teach my first Yale course, and I was already shaking.

The classroom was shaped like a bowling lane. It had a long, dark wooden table in it, with roughly four feet between the table and the walls. There was an old chalkboard that took up an entire wall and a small black monitor on a cart for displaying computer presentations such as PowerPoint slides.

The classroom was in a dingy basement and it was the tiniest room I had ever taught in. But I was teaching at Yale.

During the time before students arrived, I tried to imagine who might have sat in those seats before as well as the professors who had led seminars in this room. It was humbling.

My teaching notes were strategically set up so that I could rely heavily on them as I introduced the course. Not only was this my first time teaching a course at Yale, it was my first time teaching *this* course, Life Worth Living.

The students filed into the room excitedly. Each one was warm and very happy to be in the room. Since beginning this course, we have learned over the years that people—young and old, at Yale and far beyond the walls of Yale classrooms—have a deep desire to answer the question of what makes life worth living.

The students took seats around the table. They sat elbow to elbow given the room's size, but it did not seem to matter much to them. They looked intensely at me, each of them eager to know what I was going to say.

"Will you please stand?" I asked, and then I began to introduce the course.

"Thomas Groome writes in his book *Educating for Life*, 'To be an educator is to stand on holy ground—people's lives.'

"I say this to say that as an educator, I take your lives seriously. You have come into this space with a history full of stories and experiences that have shaped your thoughts, questions, fears, doubts, and also your desires and dreams. And all of it, all of who you are, is welcome here. I am eager to learn from you this semester as we seek to consider and answer life's most important questions. You may be seated.

"My name is Angela Gorrell. You may call me Professor Gorrell or Dr. Gorrell, if you prefer, but I do not mind if you call me Angela. I am so glad you are here."

I passed out sheets of paper with a famous poem by American poet and humanist Walt Whitman, "O Me! O Life!" and read it aloud.

9

Chapter 1

O ME! O life! . . . of the questions of these recurring;
Of the endless trains of the faithless—of cities fill'd
    with the foolish;
Of myself forever reproaching myself, (for who more
    foolish than I, and who more faithless?)
Of eyes that vainly crave the light—of the objects
    mean—of the struggle ever renew'd;
Of the poor results of all—of the plodding and sordid
    crowds I see around me;
Of the empty and useless years of the rest—with the
    rest me intertwined;
The question, O me! so sad, recurring—What good
    amid these, O me, O life?
Answer.
That you are here—that life exists, and identity;
That the powerful play goes on, and you will contribute
    a verse.

After reading the poem, I paused. Then, I looked up and scanned the room saying, "If you only hear me say one thing this semester, hear this, I believe *your life is worth living.*"

None of the students knew when I spoke these words what had happened just weeks before. They probably did not realize then that these words truly were the most important words of the semester to me.

The day after Dustin died, my husband and I drove to Kentucky early in the morning. We listened to the song "Where Rainbows Never Die" by The Steeldrivers over and over again. It became our prayer for Dustin. We were praying that he had waded through enough muddy waters, that he had no more pain, and that his mind was finally free.

We imagined him bound for glory, trading his troubles for something beautiful.

When I listen to the song, I weep. The words still resonate with my prayers. I hope he is seeing rainbows. He deserves rainbows and all of the brightest, lightest, sweetest sentiments you can think of.

Dustin, if you can read this, I wish you clear vision, the ability to see in a way that you were never able to see here. It seems your eyes might have darkened the world and made you believe that there was no goodness, no meaning, no truth, no beauty that you could recognize and connect with.

Perhaps there was a veil over everything for you and the world had become gray and dismal.

I pray you are seeing color. I hope you see yourself and the world as they are—gifts. I trust that you understand goodness, meaning, truth, and beauty in such a way that I have yet to even imagine.

All the way to Kentucky we were either talking about Dustin's life, talking about what the family was doing and thinking, talking on the phone to family members about what they were doing and thinking, listening to the song, or crying in silence.

It was the longest and shortest thirteen hours of my life.

***

Christmas weekend was anything but what we had envisioned.

Dustin was not sitting on the couch next to us playing games. Instead, he was in an urn in the seat next to me and we were driving him to his funeral. Rather than wearing red and green, we wore black.

Instead of playing games together, we took turns crying and speaking into a microphone during Dustin's funeral. Instead of sitting in rows for a group photo with laughing children on our laps, we sat in rows in a dark room with crying children on our laps.

In place of eating holiday treats in Jenna's living room, treats that we had prepared as a family, we ate soups that other people cooked. Instead of sharing holiday drinks, some of Dustin's family members and closest friends took his last bottle of bourbon to the place where he had passed away to pour it out for him.

At this point, it was late Friday night, nearly Christmas Eve.

We got out of our cars and walked to the spot. The sky was sprinkling rain when we arrived. Everyone received a small shot of Kentucky bourbon in a little paper cup. We poured one for Dustin too.

We held the cups in our fingers and talked about him, standing in a circle on the gravel parking lot under the dark sky.

We listened to his best friends talk about how much they cared for him and share some of their favorite memories. After each person spoke, they drank their little cup of bourbon. When everyone who wanted to had spoken, we poured out Dustin's cup of bourbon on the site.

Eventually the sky opened up, and rain began to pour.

I held back tears as I told the students that, no matter what they thought on this first day of class, my greatest hope was that by the end of the semester they would recognize why their lives were worth living.

There was an entire introduction to the course that I needed to get through, and this was Yale. I felt I needed to be strong—strength at that time equaled no crying—and to introduce the course well, so I went on.

"In this course, we will ask and begin to answer the most important question of our lives. *What is a life worth living?* Therefore, this is probably the most important course you will ever take. You must first come to terms with the fact that we are all amateurs when it comes to answering this question. In light of this, we are colearners this semester. You will never become an expert at the good life. However, we all have a responsibility to think about answers to this question, and *we can get better at it.* In fact, you respond to this question every day whether you intentionally wrestle with it or not. You answer this question with the relationships you invest in, the way you spend your money and your time, and the dreams that you pursue."

It was difficult to look at their young faces and not reflect on where I had been the weekend before.

I had been reading the obituary of my twenty-two-year-old nephew, Mason, at his funeral.

Just over two weeks after Dustin's funeral, while riding in the car, I received a chilling text message from my sister Jenna urging me to call her right away. Given everything that had just happened with Dustin, I was nervous to call her back. "What could it be?" I wondered. "What is so pressing?"

I called Jenna and I could not believe what I was hearing. "Mason died," she said.

Mason is the son of my oldest sister, Stefanie. I called to talk with her as soon as I got home. When I first heard Stef's voice, it was quiet. She briefly explained what happened to Mason. She sounded like she was already at a funeral and did not want to disturb the service.

Stef has a vibrant presence—a bubbly personality and booming voice. But throughout the conversation it was difficult to hear her. She sounded fragile, as if one more step might break her. Naturally, I think that at that point it was hard for her to fully grasp what had happened.

Stef explained that she had texted with Mason earlier in the week but had not heard back from him for a couple of days so she became worried. He was living in Utah and she lives in New Mexico. Over the course of three days, she kept checking her phone and seeing on the Find My Phone app that his phone was at home. After checking the app several times and learning that he had not shown up to work, she described getting a bad "mom feeling" in her gut.

Stef asked the apartment manager of Mason's complex to go check on him. The apartment manager graciously went to his apartment and knocked on his door. When he did not answer she unlocked the door with her key.

The apartment manager found him hunched over his computer keyboard.

Like Dustin, he was a gamer. Mason created video tutorials about gaming. People enjoyed listening to him comment on games while he played them. He had a following and was known as "Masonny."

Perhaps strangely, it brought us some comfort to know that Mason died while doing what he loved.

I asked Stef if I should come to New Mexico, and she softly replied, "Yes." After praying with her and hanging up I lay on my bed and sobbed. I had thought my reservoir of tears was surely empty since I had cried so much in the previous two weeks, but fresh tears were on draft.

In death, love is manifested in tears and groans.

Jenna and I planned to meet at the Atlanta airport a couple of days later and fly to New Mexico together. We were not exactly sure when the funeral would be when we booked our flights, but we knew we needed to hug Stef in person and be with her and our other sister, Allison.

Just in case, I packed the same black dress I had worn at Dustin's funeral two weeks earlier.

With Mason's youthful image in my mind, my words to the college students seemed even more urgent. I went on.

"In a few weeks, we will go on a retreat and we will think about the people and the experiences that have most shaped your vision of a life worth living. And throughout this semester we will consider how various people throughout history and living now, influenced by particular philosophical and religious traditions, have answered this question.

"The traditions that we will read about are not offering tips and tricks for making your life better. These traditions make truth claims—many of them mutually exclusive—and we're going to approach them with this assumption. If they are making truth claims about what it means to be human, what the world is, and what is worth living for, then they are making claims we each have to take seriously.

"My hope is that you will see that the constellation of truth claims made by each tradition forms a coherent whole. So this course is not ultimately a visit to a 'good life' buffet, an opportunity to mix and match willy-nilly various aspects of traditions. Nor is it a quest for the 'common core' that lies beneath or behind all of these traditions. Rather, this course is an invitation to consider deeply the claims of each tradition and the *coherent vision* of the flourishing life that they offer.

"My hope is that you will be changed by this course, through your interactions with various traditions and the people who live and have lived them and also with one another and me—that your own answers to the questions we ask this term will be refined, deepened, sharpened, and, yes, *transformed* by virtue of our time together.

"Our aim is to take seriously and read charitably the texts and the lives of people before us each week and deeply consider, 'What in life is worth wanting for yourself, your children, your family, your community?'"

The night before Life Worth Living began, only three weeks after Dustin's funeral and just days after Mason's funeral, my dad entered the story and changed everything again.

We have a beloved photo of Mason riding on Dad's shoulders during Albuquerque's annual Balloon Fiesta. Colorful hot-air balloons filled the sky, and more were on the ground waiting to take off.

In the photo, Dad and Mason are making the same face. They

are winking and they each have a hand pointing out toward the camera. They are making an "L" with their thumb and pointer finger. Dad taught Mason to wink and to do this with his hand when posing, something that was just between them, and Mason loved doing it for anyone and everyone when he was young.

Dad was wearing a bright blue fleece jacket and carrying around a silver and black camcorder, recording our reactions to the balloons and making us talk to the camera.

My grandmother, whom we affectionately called Mamaw, bought him his first camcorder in 1982. Dad *loved* to be behind a video camera. He also enjoyed talking while he was recording. It was endearing, and it is quite amusing to watch the tapes and see how much he chatted while filming. He would always say, "Flashing battery, flashing battery!" to get everyone's final wave or smile before the camera died.

At this point, he had owned many camcorders; it was 1997.

It had been several years since all four of my dad's daughters were together with him—and this was the first time we'd gathered in Albuquerque. Stef and Alli have their mom, and Jenna and I have another mom, but we all share a father, David.

Unfortunately, by this time both moms were divorced from Dad.

For a few days in October of 1997, it seemed all was right between us and our dad though.

It felt like we were getting the best of him—his jokes, his tight squeezes, and his incredibly long-winded stories. Jenna jokes that he preferred to start with Moses and work his way to the present moment when telling a story.

Dad never met a stranger.

He was the master of silly grins and had pointed eyebrows that were as black as coal. His eyebrows were positioned in a way that led you to believe he was always up to something. Jenna's son, Ro, has these same eyebrows, and whenever he looks up at us we see one of the finest, most unique parts of Dad staring back at us.

One of my favorite memories of Dad is when he played Pontius Pilate in an Easter play. It was at Jenny Wiley State Park in Kentucky. Hundreds, maybe thousands, saw the play over the several weekends it was performed. He was remarkable.

Dad wore a brilliant red gown with gold trim and a robe in an even darker shade of red. A gold band was wrapped around his head, and long golden necklaces hung from his neck. He truly looked like a king.

His perfectly trimmed jet-black beard and pointed jet-black eyebrows greatly added to the look. He even wore black eyeliner. While playing his part, his voice rumbled throughout the outdoor amphitheater and made the hairs stand up on our arms. Dad was bold and convincing. The audience loved him, and I did too.

I was really proud of him.

Our dad lived *BIG* most of his life—all or nothing. At age five, he jumped from a barn and broke not one, but both arms. And he broke both arms *again* not long after they had healed. He played every sport his high school offered and played them well. His senior yearbook, *The Pirate*, has countless photos of him strewn throughout, with captions like "Williams gets set to drive" and "Williams makes a Touchdown!"

He was a big-time lawyer at one point, chalking up nothing but wins in the courtroom. He would pace and pause intentionally in front of jurors during his opening and closing remarks. It seemed like he held the members of the jury in the palm of his hand. He wore a sharp suit nearly every day no matter where he was going or what he was doing.

He walked big, danced big, sang and played the guitar big, partied big, and most importantly, he loved big.

This big love, as is the case in any relationship, was imperfect in many ways. Our dad's series of four marriages and life choices had made it difficult for any of his four daughters to have a sustained, deep relationship with him, especially in recent years.

When I was in my early twenties, I started to notice that Dad sounded sleepy on the phone. When I would call him, he would slur his words and his sentences would run together like he had been put under anesthesia and was about to go into surgery. Sometimes he even fell asleep on the phone and I would have to hang up and wait to talk to him until another day.

Initially, I was confused.

"Why is Dad so sleepy all of the time?" I wondered.

I thought maybe it was because he stayed up too late at night.

And he often did; he had always been a night owl. I thought he was just exhausted.

But over the years, I realized that it was happening with more frequency.

And then Dad began to forget what we had talked about during the sleepy conversations. I would have to remind him of what we had last discussed. I would have to tell the same story three times.

Eventually, he stopped going to work and wearing suits. He barely showered.

Things progressively got worse. He forgot what city I lived in, where I worked, and the name of my graduate school. Over time, my confusion turned into sadness; and after several years of sleepy conversations I got really angry.

I was angry that he could not remember important details about my life, angry that I had to tell him significant stories multiple times, angry that the man who once was so enthusiastic about what I was doing either could not stay awake for our phone calls or did not answer at all.

It seems so obvious now, especially when I consider the symptoms of opioid addiction: drowsiness, nodding off, insomnia, memory impairment, a loss of interest in grooming and personal appearance, reduced participation in activities that were once enjoyed, neglect of responsibilities, and withdrawal from family and friends.

As the saying goes, hindsight is 20/20.

I passed out index cards to my Life Worth Living students after explaining that I wanted to give them a gift that semester. I told them I wanted to give them the gift of doing just one thing: being present to one another in respectful dialogue about life's most fundamental questions.

"Too many of us do not embrace this gift," I remarked. "We do not know how to be truly present to others, especially not in respectful discussion, and most especially not about life's biggest questions."

I told them each to write on one side of the index card their answer to this question: "What are some things you want to lay down to be more present this semester?" And on the other side of the card they were invited to write an answer to the question: "Where do you hope this experience will take you?"

I filled out my own index card.

I wrote down Dustin, Mason, and Dad on both sides. It was actually impossible to do the very thing I was asking students to do. I could not do just one thing. I could not just be present to the moment and introduce the class. Too much had happened. Too much was happening.

And what could I possibly long for at that point?

I just hoped that somehow over the coming months my family would find the strength, the mercy, to get out of bed every day.

I also asked the students to put symbols on their cards that would allow them to identify the cards later and then put their cards into a wooden box that I would keep at my home.

We passed the box around the table and everyone put their cards inside.

Afterward, the students were asked to introduce themselves to one another. They were to say their name, one thing they were good at, why they wanted to take Life Worth Living, and where they considered home. I mentioned it could be a special lake or perhaps their answer might be that they do not consider anywhere to be home.

I was stunned by how easily they shared, and I was genuinely moved by their responses. While listening to them talk, it was increasingly obvious that this was going to be unlike any other course I had taught.

About ten o'clock the night before my first day of teaching Life Worth Living, I was preparing to go to bed when I noticed I had a message.

The message read: "Angela. David was taken to the hospital. He is very weak. The doctor said he may not make it through the night."

I felt numb.

I had not even recovered from my trip to Kentucky for Dustin's funeral, not to mention New Mexico. I had just gotten home from Mason's funeral two days earlier. I slept so little the previous days that it was hard to even comprehend what she was saying.

I was so bogged down by my grief about Dustin and Mason that it was impossible to imagine my heart could break further. Plus, my dad seemingly had nine lives. I had been called several times during the previous decade and told to come see my dad because he was about to die.

I thought, "Surely my dad is not dying this week."

I was an exhausted, depleted, nervous wreck, so I told Paul about the message and immediately explained that I had to go to sleep because I had to go to the first class of Life Worth Living, my first class as a teacher at Yale.

I quickly got into bed and pulled the covers up close to my face.

Reflecting back, these were survival techniques. I probably would have had an emotional breakdown if I had thought more about that message that night.

The next morning, I got dressed and put on makeup and pretended like this was not the first class I had taught at Yale and this was certainly not the first time I had taught Life Worth Living. I taught as if Dustin had not just died by suicide and I had not just been at my young nephew's funeral.

Until the very end of the class, I even taught as if my dad was not in the ICU fighting for his life.

Right before I dismissed class, I casually mentioned that my dad was sick in the hospital and that if I was not present for the next class session, it would be because I was visiting him in Kentucky.

2

Hooked

Nothing's more powerful than the morphine molecule, and once it has its hooks in you, nothing matters more. Not love. Not family. Not sex. Not shelter. The only relationship that matters is between you and the drug.

—Beth Macy, *Dopesick*

DJ's slow death was caught on camera at his workplace. His heroin dealer brought him the drugs while he was making and selling doughnuts. DJ had been trying to change his life. He had a job and a place to live. He even had months of recovery and sobriety under his belt. He wanted things to be different.

His journal includes a page dedicated to the sentence, "I can do this." He was referring to sobriety. The sentence was written over and over again in black ink.

But the desire for the effect of the drug was strong.

DJ's childhood friend brought heroin hidden inside a dollar bill to the doughnut shop where he was working. DJ went to the back of the shop and snorted some of it and injected more of it in the bathroom, wearing his baker's pants.

Video footage shows DJ about twenty minutes later rocking back and forth while glazing doughnuts. Slowly, his body moved forward until half of his body was lying over the doughnuts on the counter.

A coworker tried twice to wake DJ up while he was lying over the counter. Both times, after being unable to wake him, she went back to doing her job. Two customers came to the store and could see DJ lying on the counter but did nothing. Perhaps they did not know what to do. Perhaps they did not think something was wrong.

Finally, DJ's manager arrived at the shop, saw him, and dialed 911. But it was too late. DJ was dead. What DJ had thought was merely heroin was in fact fentanyl.

Fentanyl—an opioid that can be integrated into multiple substances—is the most deadly synthetic opioid that has ever been created. Fentanyl is fifty to a hundred times stronger than morphine.

Prince, the music icon who created memorable songs like "Purple Rain," suffered a similar fate as DJ—though the two men's lives are otherwise incomparable.

On April 21, 2016, Prince was found alone and unresponsive in an elevator at his home, Paisley Park. There was an exceedingly high concentration of fentanyl in his stomach and liver.

Chapter 2

At just five feet two, Prince was a force of nature—he dabbled in multiple genres and redefined those genres in the process: pop, rock, R&B, funk, and soul. He wrote and produced his own music, topped music charts, won Grammys and an Oscar, and performed on stages across the United States and around the globe. Prince's music career was filled with engaging, high energy performances, and that meant he suffered countless injuries and was in significant physical pain.

He was prescribed opioid pain pills.

In the days before his death, he thought he was taking Vicodin, an often-prescribed pain pill containing an opioid, but accidentally took counterfeit pills laced with fentanyl instead.

Upon investigation, numerous pills were discovered in Prince's home. The day before he died, Prince's team had contacted an opioid-addiction specialist.

Overlooking the opioid crisis is relatively easy until you are surprised to find yourself drawn to the comfortable escape of opioids or until you discover it is your loved one who is secretly addicted.

That's when worlds get turned upside down.

———

Dad lived in Appalachia on a valley road in between two mountains. We call these kinds of roads "hollers" in Kentucky. So Dad lived up a holler—in a trailer.

It was two and a half hours from the city where Mom, Jenna, and I lived after their divorce, and after I moved to California it became more and more difficult to visit him there. It was not only because visiting from out of state required at least two planes plus the two-and-a-half-hour drive in a borrowed car, but because over time Dad's addiction to opioids destroyed his life.

His opioid of choice was Percocet. Percocet contains a combination of Acetaminophen and the highly addictive opioid oxycodone, which, taken in large quantities, causes liver damage.

After a couple of hip surgeries, Dad received disability benefits that covered opioids for pain. The move in the mid-1980s to
replace welfare payments with disability benefits together with
the opioid surge in the 1990s paired perfectly to allow pharma-
ceutical companies and doctors to make astonishing amounts of
money while people who became addicted to pain pills withdrew
from life and drew disability instead.

Over the years, the effects of the pills on Dad's life became
more and more severe. In 2012, Paul and I went to visit him on
Christmas Day. Paul had never met him, and it was important
to me that they have a conversation in person. In my mind I had
always imagined both of my parents having a meaningful relationship with whomever I married. I knew my relationship with
Paul was serious and that marriage was a possibility.

But I was terrified to take Paul to Dad's house.

I was afraid of what state it would be in and how Dad would
look, and I was nervous about what he might say. I did my best
to prepare Paul for what he was about to encounter.

I told him the house would likely be messy and Dad was long-
winded without much to talk about—a nerve-racking, often frustrating combination.

I explained that Dad lived near some family members who
helped him sometimes, but that I did not know them well and
it was all incredibly complicated. I told Paul that Dad had not
had a job in a while and did not get out much, and that I was
not sure what sort of food or drinks he would have around, even
at Christmas.

Paul and I stopped by the only open store on the main road
about forty minutes from Dad's house to buy two frozen pizzas.
We took him a Christmas card and a couple of gifts to open.
I remember that night so vividly, but I am not exactly sure what
gift we took him to open—maybe a western film on DVD. I do
remember telling Paul that Dad loved Christmas.

It had always been his favorite time of year.

For Dad, Christmastime was for playing Christmas songs on
the guitar and bellowing "Ho ho ho!" everywhere he went, just
to embarrass us.

Chapter 2

Dad would wear a Santa hat for weeks before Christmas Day. Christmas was a time for eating abundant amounts of food and dessert and opening lots of presents, usually silly gifts that no one needed, such as stuffed animals that danced and sang. Dad would decorate the entire house in lights. He loved to use strands with huge bright bulbs.

Paul and I had a hard time finding Dad's house in the dark.

There were no Christmas lights on the outside of the trailer to set it apart. And the holler had no streetlights. His house had no mailbox, and our cell phones had lost service. But after slowing down significantly and looking carefully, I recognized his house, which sat in a pool of mud and gravel just off the road. It had a wooden ramp that a group from Habitat for Humanity built for him so he could be pushed in his wheelchair to and from his car.

I knocked on the door several times, but no one answered. It was freezing and we had driven a long way, so I decided to walk inside.

Immediately inside, just to my right sat three open bags of garbage.

Between them and the walls of the would-be living room, various household objects were in piles all over the floor. I turned to close the door behind Paul and noticed it was being held together by duct tape.

"Hello? Dad?"

I called out to him as we walked into the area where his dining room table was, an old wooden thing with a variety of mismatched chairs around it. He slowly came through the kitchen in his wheelchair, wearing a baggy tee shirt and flannel pajama pants. He had lost a lot of weight. Dad immediately put his right hand through his thinning dark hair and muttered that he had not showered in a few days and was surprised to see us.

"Merry Christmas! We brought pizza," I exclaimed, trying to cover up all of the awkwardness (and my great sadness) with Christmas joy.

I mentioned that I had tried to call.

"Hi. Good to see you. I'm Paul," Paul said, sticking out his hand. Dad looked dazed but pulled his wheelchair to the table, and Paul sat next to him.

I was so nervous that I started preparing the pizzas for the oven. I had no idea what we were all going to talk about or how to ignore the state of the house. I knew something was wrong, but I felt ill equipped to respond. I felt like I should help him, but over the years I had felt more and more powerless.

Anyone who has loved someone struggling with addiction knows this feeling of powerlessness.

I opened the fridge to discover that all of the shelves were sideways. And much of the food inside was spoiled. Everything in the kitchen was very dirty. There were dishes all over the counters and in the sink.

I found a pan and heated up the pizzas. We used thin white paper plates and paper towels while eating our slices.

It is not as if I needed the lights, the Santa hat, the silly gifts, the guitar, the spread of food, or the bellowing voice shouting "Ho ho ho!" for it to be Christmas. But the absence of all of these things, with frozen pizza on paper plates in their place, was a nearly unbearable metaphor for all that we had lost in recent years.

At one point during the visit, Paul had to go to the bathroom. He walked through the kitchen and through a narrow doorway, and Dad and I talked while he was away. Upon his return, his face told me I needed to see what he had just seen. Paul asked if there was somewhere to wash his hands. He was told the water was not turned on but that he could adjust the settings under the sink in the kitchen to wash his hands there—above the filthy pile of dishes.

I walked through the kitchen to the bathroom and immediately discovered it no longer had a door. The bathtub and the shower were both filled with random objects from the house, and the tile floor was covered in dirt.

I was shocked.

It was hard to wrap my mind around Dad's housing situation. How could the man who had worn suits daily, charmed audiences, and led church youth groups be living this way? I needed to use the bathroom too, so I made my way to the other side of the house. There I found the washer was open, not running but filled to the brim with murky water and clothing that smelled sour after days of sitting stagnant.

I shuffled past it, trying not to take in the smell, and entered the other bathroom only to discover its sink was overflowing with empty pill bottles.

You may wonder how it could have taken me years to realize my dad was addicted to prescription opioids. The truth is that I don't know exactly why it took so long. All of the signs were there.

I think it was difficult to equate his use of pills with misuse because Dad *did* have significant pain. He had two hip replacement surgeries and other medical problems. He could always tell me something new that needed to be fixed or needed to be managed by a doctor. Basically, I just kept believing he needed the pills and resigned myself to the idea that he was never going to be who he used to be.

Several years into using opioid pills, he seemed to give up on pursuing actual healing. He never did what he needed to do after hip surgery to rehabilitate fully, for example. For over a decade he never stopped using opioids and seemed to use more and more. In the process he acquired a new vocation, a new rhythm of life centered on pain and opioids.

I do not know whether Dad fully realized he had become dependent on the pills he was taking.

In other words, I do not know whether he would identify as someone addicted to prescription pills rather than as someone who needed to take large amounts of medicine every day to survive. I think he may have convinced himself that pills were the only cure for his pain. And I imagine that over time he became unable to tell the difference between pain caused by existing ailments and pain caused by opioid withdrawal.

Dad went from being a capable, dapper attorney who would not be caught without a suit on to a needy, navel-gazing person hooked on pain pills.

It is hard to conceptualize just how widespread and destructive the opioid crisis is. But this might help. The average person reads 200 to 250 words per minute. You have likely been reading this chapter for about eleven minutes. If so, since you began reading, at least one person has died from an opioid overdose.

It was excruciating to see the man who always lived *BIG* live so small. Dad went from buying everyone dinner at restaurants—he was the life of the party—to hardly ever leaving his house, sometimes not leaving his bedroom for multiple days. He was constantly whispering on the phone because "people might be listening in," incessantly quoting televangelists, and feeling paranoid that everyone was out to take things from him.

It does make sense that he worried about his things being stolen.

People had stripped his trailer of multiple parts, such as pipes from underneath the house. It is possible these things were stolen to get money for drugs; stealing random house parts and objects in yards—like lawnmowers—to exchange for money is a documented phenomenon, especially in rural areas.

Dad obsessed over his ailments, diagnosing himself constantly and explaining all the surgeries he needed to be well again.

Yet he went to doctors only to get more pain medicine, never to actually get well. Dad went to so many doctors over twelve years of abusing opioids that eventually he was driving over an hour to meet with doctors who would fill his prescriptions.

The rates of opioid prescription since the 1990s are mind-boggling. In 2017, for example, doctors in Kentucky (where Dad lived) prescribed at a rate of 86.8 prescriptions for every 100 people—one of the highest prescription rates in the country. In Alabama, which had the highest rate, doctors wrote 107.2 prescriptions per 100 people.

That's right, more than one opioid prescription was written *per person* that year in Alabama.

How did this happen?

For one thing, people could simply tell a doctor they were in pain; for another, for decades the go-to solution for pain in America has been prescription opioids—especially when the pain is deemed time-consuming to resolve or is viewed as too labor-intensive or expensive to cure because it necessitates physical and psychological therapy.

It seems too many doctors and too many of us have become satisfied with numbing pain rather than seeking true healing.

Dad's Bible reveals that anxiety was a major contributor to his cycles of pill misuse.

The cover is navy blue leather, worn-out from years of use. It's the Amplified Bible version—fitting for a lover of long, drawn out sentences, thick descriptions, and verbal processing.

As his daughter who loves to talk like he did, I get it.

This version of the Bible stops in places to use multiple adjectives or other types of words to say the same thing over and over again but in varied ways so you really get what the author is trying to express. Throughout the pages, he has dates and little notes in black pen. Sometimes the notes even contain the time he was writing.

At 7:15 a.m. on November 15, 2013, he starred Psalm 94:19, a verse about how God's comfort cheers and delights the soul despite a multitude of anxious thoughts.

In numerous places in his Bible, especially in 2013, Dad wrote prayers asking God to help him with his anxiety. Lots of people can relate. No one wants to feel overwhelmed with anxiety.

The thing is, anxiety contributes to an especially vicious cycle when opioids are involved. Opioids numb the ills of anxiety for a little while. Opioids can actually feel like they are providing relief for worried, troubled, and nervous hearts; that is likely why people use opioids and want to keep using them.

Yet after the high wears off, opioid withdrawal generates and stokes anxiety. Withdrawal makes people feel anxious, and if one is low on supply the need to find the next fix only adds to this anxiety.

During phone calls, Dad was always quoting the Bible and

talking about how God was doing this or that in his life—how God was going to heal him and help him, how God had plans for him. Dad always believed in God and believed God was good.

Whenever I told him I needed to get off the phone, he prayed really long prayers. When I say long prayers, I mean ten-minute prayers. I mean I could put down the phone, put him on speaker, and curl my hair while he was praying. It's as if he knew this was a good way to keep me in the conversation.

Who would dare interrupt a prayer?

Dad wanted to keep talking to me, but I also think he really enjoyed praying and felt like it was something meaningful he could do for me. On many days his faith genuinely moved me.

Yet there were also days I was less moved by his devotion to God and more annoyed with his seemingly blatant hypocrisy. I did not get why my dad could be so down with Jesus while simultaneously so down with being high as a kite.

I think Dad's theology frustrated me because I thought he was more interested in God's agency than his own.

So during certain calls his prayers sounded like nails on a chalkboard—like painful and unnecessary noise. Sometimes his Bible quoting and preaching became occasions that deepened my bitterness. I imagine—I couldn't help but imagine despite all my sincere beliefs to the contrary—that his addiction to pills had made him unfit for such discussions.

I think I unknowingly (and wrongly) believed his addiction to opioids was a moral failure. Then, somehow despite all I had learned about God's unconditional love I mistakenly also believed moral failure had levels and his level of moral failure meant he should not be talking to me about God.

I remember the first time my dad forgot my birthday. He did not send a card and did not call. I remember being baffled, imagining that in the days to come he would suddenly recall that he had missed the day and call me apologizing. I honestly cannot recollect if he ever remembered it that year and called me to apologize. But I know that this became a pattern. All of a sudden he just stopped remembering my birthday.

Maybe it was not so much that he could not remember what day I was born but rather that he just stopped knowing which day it was.

This neglect of important days in my life should have prepared me for my wedding, but it didn't. I got married in San Diego but decided to have a reception in Lexington, Kentucky, where I lived from eight to eighteen years old. I made sure we had this event (which my aunt Teri and uncle Chris graciously hosted) just so Dad could experience wedding joy with me and Paul.

I gave him several months of notice. I told him in April that we were coming to Lexington in October.

All he needed to do was get to my aunt's house.

Every time we talked between April and October, I reminded him of my wedding reception and asked him to make preparations so he could be there. I told him over and over again how much I looked forward to us dancing together, that his wheelchair would be fine, and that he could easily get to the backyard. We talked about which family members could bring him. We discussed how he would come and how wonderful it would be.

I told him all of the details about the special day, and though I knew somehow in the deepest parts of my soul that he might not come I was almost positive that he would not miss this, not my wedding reception.

It was too important.

I called Dad on the morning of the reception. He muttered something about his car not working well and that he had no other ride. He was really sorry, but he was not going to make it.

Another Christmas, I went with Jenna and our husbands to check on Dad. Dad actually called Jenna and me asking for help.

We had in mind that we would take him to an assisted-living facility. Ever since Paul and I had seen the state he was in three years earlier, we had been praying that we would be able to help him. It seemed he was now ready for us to intervene.

For weeks before Christmastime in 2015, we had numerous phone calls with him and planned how to help him. He had convinced the two of us that his safety was in jeopardy. Several phone calls were made to the state and even to Adult Protective Services because of fear for Dad's health and well-being.

Jenna was the main orchestrator of the plan to help Dad since she has the education and skills as an occupational therapist to help people recover from pain and get their lives back. While working full time, Jenna spent multiple lunch breaks placed on hold listening to elevator music. She spent evenings sitting behind closed doors—under which little baby fingers slipped in search of mommy—saying, "just one more minute" while she endlessly called facilities to find a placement for him and gathered information about a Medicaid application.

Jenna even mailed him paperwork ahead of time and lovingly explained every detail to prepare him for this transition. I marveled at what she had done; I was confident that this transition was going to change his life.

3

Too Late

A healthy soul, therefore, must do two things for us. First, it must put some fire in our veins, keep us energized, vibrant, living with zest, and full of hope as we sense that life is, ultimately, beautiful and worth living. Whenever this breaks down in us, something is wrong with our souls. When cynicism, despair, bitterness, or depression paralyze our energy, part of the soul is hurting. Second, a healthy soul has to keep us fixed together. It has to continually give us a sense of who we are, where we came from, where we are going, and what sense there is in all of this. When we stand looking at ourselves, confusedly, in a mirror and ask ourselves what sense, if any, there is to our lives, it is this other part of the soul, our principle of integration, that is limping.

—Ronald Rolheiser,
The Holy Longing

We arrived at Dad's house, and when he saw us—even though it was Christmas and we had not seen him in months and had been showing him compassion for weeks on the phone—he immediately wheeled toward us and sternly asked, "Did you bring it? Did you? The medical card? The card I sent you in the mail? It has money on it. I need to activate it, then let's get in the car. Can you take me to the store? The pharmacy has my prescriptions there."

No hello. No Merry Christmas. No hugs.

In fact, he was much more troubled, anxious, and mean than he had been the first time he met Paul. He said he wanted his bag of pills and his benefits card and he wanted to get out of his house and go to the pharmacy to get more pills.

Dad's bag of pills was a large black leather bag that zipped down the center. The zipper was broken from the bag being over-stuffed with prescription bottles and years and years of overuse. He would unzip and rezip it frequently each day, even when he was not getting anything out of it.

When we asked him where he planned to go after the pharmacy, he talked about the facility. We told him that he would not need pills there because they would have medicine for him. But Dad said that he would not go to the facility without taking his bag of pills with him and picking up more on the way.

Since my sister worked near the facility where we had planned to take him, he thought she could simply sneak the pills to him whenever he needed extra. He explained that the facility would not be able to manage his pain the way he could.

When he refused to go to the facility without his black leather gym bag of pills, I grew infuriated inside but tried to remain calm on the outside.

At the time I did not understand what he knew.

Anyone who has been addicted to pills and knows what happens when you go without them would understand where Dad was coming from. Withdrawal from opioids causes paralyzing nervousness, extreme diarrhea, intense cramping, and sweating.

It is referred to as being dopesick.

In hindsight, I remember Dad's pale body breaking into sweats on various occasions. He had always been someone who sweats a lot when working out or even wearing a suit on a hot day. But looking back, I realize the sweating in the last few years of his life was different.

When I visited him for an extended period of time his skin would grow clammy. In those last years of visits, he did not go out in the sun. He would barely move while wearing a baggy t-shirt in moderate home temperatures, and yet the sweating would come on.

We tried talking with Dad.

We got him to come to the living room and sit in a circle with us. We asked him if he had filled out the paperwork and packed. Even though he had done neither, we still tried to move the conversation in the direction of preparing him to go to the facility. We enthusiastically told him how much it would help him and how great it would be.

But he was not having it.

He wanted us to take him to the pharmacy and then drop him off at a motel. He no longer wanted to be in his house on that holler. But he did not want to go to the facility either. He no longer wanted to discuss getting surgery to cure his hip pain or getting physical and occupational therapy.

He just wanted his pills, and he mysteriously imagined that being alone at peace in a motel room would be the magic solution to all of his problems.

We had no intention of taking him to a motel, but we wanted to keep talking to him to see if the lack of logic in his vision would finally dawn on him. When we asked how he would get food (given that he could no longer drive and had very little money) he said that every once in a while he would get a taxi to take him to a gas station so he could buy snacks.

Honestly, while the taxi part was unimaginable, given how much help he needed to get around and get in and out of vehicles, the part about living off of Little Debbie snacks from the gas station was not out of the question.

He lived for honey buns and oatmeal cream pies.

We sat there dumbfounded, looking at each other, trying to understand where the sensible part of him had gone. Where was the Dad we had known all our lives? He had a lot of education. He knew how to be logical. And he said he loved us. Why could he not see what we could see? Why didn't he want our help? Why did he think sitting alone in a motel room was better than getting well, better than being with us?

Why didn't he want to be able to see Jenna every day and get his life back?

The conversation took a dramatic, painful turn.

Even though it was Christmas and we had only been at his house a couple of hours, Dad began saying mean things about and to Jenna. She was the person in the room who knew the most about how to help him, and she insisted that he could not take his pills with him and needed to fill out paperwork that would give his disability stipend to his care rather than pills. Because of that, she became his scapegoat.

To Dad, Jenna was not a person trying to rescue him. She was a person trying to keep him from what he wanted most.

In a conversation I had a few years later with Trevor, Nashville's Opioid Response Coordinator, one thing he said really struck me.

He said that when he asked people who were addicted to opioids about what it did for them, they responded that it made them feel loved.

And then he asked rhetorically, "How do you compete with a drug that makes people feel loved?"

Hurt and helpless, we all looked at each other and without speaking recognized that we had to leave. The situation was getting worse by the minute. We realized that even though he had acted as though he was open to change for weeks before this day and had actively asked for help, he was not going to accept it unless it meant having money for and access to his prescription pills.

It was too late.

We could not save someone who did not want saving.

Chapter 3

The morning after my first day of teaching Life Worth Living, I woke up to the doorbell ringing. I walked downstairs, opened the door, and found a box of groceries on my front porch that had just been delivered. Inside there were pita chips and all sorts of other snacks. A group of my best girlfriends in Los Angeles sent me the box of goodies to tell me they were thinking of me and praying.

Upon hearing about my dad being in the hospital, one of them sprang into action and rallied all of my friends together to send me that incredible gift. It felt like a hug from three thousand miles away.

I had been up late the night before debating whether I should go see Dad. I found out he had pneumonia and his liver and kidneys were shutting down. After years of pills, they were worn out.

I decided to call Phil, the managing director of the center where I worked. I was sitting on my bed crying, and I asked him whether he thought I should go. He said the sentence I needed to hear: He told me not to think about it any longer and to buy a ticket and get on a plane as soon as possible.

If someone calls you crying and asking whether they should go see someone they love who is dying, be the gift that Phil was to me that day. Give them permission to drop everything and do it. Tell them everything else will work itself out.

I booked my flights. It was going to take three planes and a rental car to get to my dad in rural Kentucky. I had about thirty minutes until I needed to leave. I started throwing things into a carry-on, packing the same black dress I wore at Dustin's and Mason's funerals.

At the last minute, Paul decided he needed to come with me. I still thank God that he had the wisdom to make this decision. I don't know how I would have made it without him. We had to buy a ticket at the airport because the flight was leaving forty-five minutes later, and it was too late to buy online.

40

(A few weeks later, Phil left a check in an envelope on my desk at work that paid for both of our plane tickets. Phil's compassion and generosity in those weeks is etched on my heart.)

We boarded the first plane, and since we had booked our flights that morning we were not sitting next to each other. I cried through the entire flight. It is impossible to know what the stranger in the seat next to me thought. Maybe she didn't notice.

On the second plane, I was in the last group that was called (again, our late booking meant we had no early check-in). The flight attendants said my luggage had to be checked in. Paul's bag was going to fit in the cabin, but mine had to go under. I explained that I needed my bag with me, that my dad was dying and important things were inside. But the flight attendants insisted they had to take it and that everything would be fine.

I panicked and cried even more.

I (barely) managed to sit down before losing my self-control. I could have easily become hysterical, but I did not want to be taken off the plane. I knew how it worked out in the movies.

On the third and final plane, I cried even more. When someone asked if I was okay, I told them my dad was dying, which was a conversation stopper. It is difficult to know what to say in the face of death. On the other hand, maybe they just understood that there are no sufficient words in the last hours of a parent's life. We landed at the small airport in Huntington, West Virginia, and waited for my bag.

It never came.

So my dad was dying and I was standing at the lost luggage counter with two guys who looked a few days over eighteen. I just couldn't keep it together anymore. I sobbed and angrily told them I knew this would happen. I told them that if they ever found my bag they needed to bring it to a hospital in the next state over where I would be witnessing my dad's death.

They did what any terrified teen would do when faced with a sobbing woman at the luggage counter and swore to God they would get it to me the next day—and then likely filed their two weeks' notices.

Chapter 3

Paul lovingly told me he would fill out the paperwork and get the rental car. He had me sit on a bench and wait for him. He knew I was incapable of being helpful to myself or anyone else at this point. Like I said, thank God he came with me.

After what felt like forever, we started driving to the hospital. It was still going to be over an hour before we could get to Dad. It was after nine at night. Paul drove through the mountains of Appalachia, and I just kept crying. Jenna called me about an hour into the drive.

"He's not doing well," she said. "They think he is going to die soon." I called his hospital room and asked a family member to put their cell phone close to one of Dad's ears.

"I'm coming, Daddy. I will be there in just a few minutes. I love you. Please don't go. I will see you soon."

I became hysterical. I had to see him. Paul put on the car's flashers and drove as fast as possible, running red lights. Jenna and I kept calling each other. We were both fully panicking.

"We aren't going to make it, are we?"

"Oh God, we have to make it in time. Drive fast. Please, please drive fast. Oh God."

When we arrived at the hospital, I was so terrified that I basically jumped out of the car before Paul could even try to find a place to park. I had no idea where I was going, but I was running. I ran to several desks at the hospital to figure out which floor to go to. I had not thought to find out where his room was exactly before arriving.

I ran through several hallways and cried in the elevator as it was making its way to his floor. "Why didn't I find the stairs?" I thought.

When I finally found his room and walked in, Dad's eyes were the only things he could still move. His mouth was open and dry. Even his tongue was paralyzed. I watched his gaze move back and forth, from the right side of the hospital bed to the left.

He saw me.

His eyes could track my movements and when he realized who I was, tears fell down his cheeks. Simultaneously, tears fell down mine. "It's okay, Daddy," I quietly said through my whimpers. "I'm here. Angela is here. I love you."

His breathing was shallow, and his skin was yellow. His feet had turned blue, and his toes had already begun to die.

There's something about having a parent die that takes you back to being a little child.

I felt like my youngest, neediest self.

I wanted to be as close to him as humanly possible. I rubbed his hair. I touched his face and shoulders and arms and hands. I gently caressed his arms while crying.

Miraculously, Jenna arrived about five minutes after I did. Jenna and I sang to him, songs he had sung to us all of our lives. We also played hymns for him on our cell phones, and when he heard them he cried, and we cried too. He was especially moved by the song "It Is Well." Tears flowed down his cheeks.

I knew then that he was ready for what was next.

He wanted to leave this life and enter into more life. We also played "Amazing Grace," "Blessed Assurance," "Great Is Thy Faithfulness," "In the Garden," "Precious Lord, Take My Hand," "How Great Thou Art," "Just as I Am," and "Turn Your Eyes upon Jesus."

It was appropriate to send him on with music.

He loved to play the guitar and had sung all of his life. I remember watching him on the stage at Immanuel Baptist Church singing during worship services and in the church basement singing for the youth group.

I held his hand for nearly five hours.

I could not bring myself to let go of his hand except to run (literally) to the restroom twice during that five hours. I wanted to be present for every second of the last moments of his life. I did not want to miss his last breath or heartbeat. I did not want him to be scared or to be without me.

Everything that had separated us in the previous years— addiction and with it stubbornness, money, sickness, distance, heartache—could not get in the way of that sacred night.

We read to him too. We read biblical passages that he had loved for years, ones that he read to us as children, like Proverbs

3:5–6: "Trust in the Lord with all your heart and lean not on your own understanding; in all your ways submit to him, and he will make your paths straight." We also read him verses that would help him to feel loved, like a portion of Romans 8: "Who will separate us from the love of Christ?" We reminded him of Psalm 139, telling him he was fearfully and wonderfully made and that no darkness would keep God's light from him, for even darkness is as light to God.

The hardest verses of all to read were those of Psalm 23. He was indeed walking through the valley of the shadow of death. But we wanted him to know he was not alone and had no reason to fear.

We recited the Lord's Prayer and read a blessing over him, too.

> The Lord bless you
> and keep you;
> the Lord make his face shine on you
> and be gracious to you;
> the Lord turn his face toward you
> and give you peace.

We whispered things to him and also talked openly to him. We told him about Jenna's pregnancy. She put his hand on her stomach and told him she was having a boy, and she said she hoped he had Dad's features.

We reminded Dad of the best times. We exchanged sorries about the hardest times. We told him over and over that he was not alone, that he was okay, and that we loved him. We named out loud whom he would see when he got to heaven, like his mom and siblings and grandson, Mason. We tried to imagine with him what it would be like when he met Jesus, whom he loved with all his heart.

I remember wondering how I was supposed to sound full of hope and joy while my heart was breaking.

In the hardest moments of all, we told him he could go and

that we would miss him dearly but that we understood. We told him we did not want him to suffer anymore.

At about 1:45 a.m., Dad's breathing became more difficult. The nurse came in and said he was nearing the end and that she would be back more frequently to check on us and keep him comfortable.

He started taking a lot more time between breaths, and we became unsure whether he would take many more. We had known this was going to happen, but we were still unprepared. Suddenly Jenna screamed out, a cross between a desperate cry of anguish and uncontrollable weeping.

Dad was so startled that he took a long, deep breath in.

My sister had shocked him back to life with her grief. To this day we assume he stayed alive a couple of hours more for his youngest daughter. He could not bear to hear her be so sad to lose him.

Jenna realized that she needed to give him permission to die, that he needed to know she would be all right so he could go in peace. Right there by that hospital bed she displayed more courage than I had ever seen her exhibit before. In a soft, compassionate, tearless voice she told him that she was sorry she scared him and, again, that she was going to miss him terribly but that he could go. She told him she understood, and she promised him that she was going to be okay.

It was holy ground.

We watched him take his last breaths. I counted the seconds between them. They went from one-second intervals to ten to seventeen to eighteen to twenty-one—until it was more like forty—and then I just kept whispering, "It's okay, Daddy. I send my love to you." I said it over and over again.

After he took his last breath, I counted and counted and then realized there would not be another. I laid my head over his body and wept. I got on my knees and placed my hands on the cold tile floor and begged God to have mercy on him, on us.

Dad died about 3:45 a.m.

When he took his final breath, Jenna stayed quiet. She made

sure he was really gone before saying anything or expressing her emotions. She did not want to startle him again. Just as we had hoped for Dustin just three weeks earlier, she wanted Dad to be free.

Once she realized he was truly gone, she lay over him and her own breathing became stifled. She could barely take in enough oxygen to keep crying. I have never wanted so badly to heal someone's pain and yet known so clearly that it was impossible to do so.

The nurses gave Dad a bath, changed his attire, and lovingly folded the blankets that had been over him. What an incredible gift nurses are, especially those who courageously and lovingly walk with us in the final hours. Afterward, we had the chance to see him again.

It was difficult to give him one last hug and kiss, and heart-rending to walk away for the last time.

Exhausted, we made our way to a nearby hotel sometime around 6:00 a.m. We tried to sleep for a few hours, but it was incredibly difficult. I decided to get out of bed and shower. I wanted to clean my face and wash my oily hair.

Usually, I enjoy showers. The water rushing down my back feels like a long, hard day is going down the drain. This shower was different.

I stepped into the large shower and in my exhausted state had forgotten to turn on the bathroom light, so the stall was dark. As the water poured over my face and over me, I suddenly felt an urgent need to cry hard. I had cried in the moments after Dad's death as I knelt beside his hospital bed, but I realized in the midst of the water that there was a previously unknown kind of grief welling up in me that desperately needed to be let out. This grief was way down, somewhere in the pit of my stomach. Or rather, my soul.

I began gushing tears with heaving sobs.

In the darkness where I was alone and felt free, I let it go. I cried loudly and violently. After who knows how long, when there were literally no more tears to release, I got out of the shower, dried off and wrapped a towel around myself. I walked into the room where Paul was and sat on the edge of the bed.

"I cried in the shower," I said casually.

Naively, I had believed that the bathroom wall was a safety barrier between my pain and Paul's ears. Paul gently explained that he had heard me and that it was impossible not to. I was too tired to be embarrassed.

I put on the same clothes I had worn for twenty-four hours, but as we headed out of the hotel I discovered my carry-on had just arrived. Either the airport gods smiled down upon me or the young men I had terrified with my desperation at the lost luggage counter quit their jobs and drove it right to me as soon as it came on the next plane.

Thankful for fresh clothes, I dressed, and we began making our way to Dad's house—that is, the house he had been living in most recently. Jenna and Rob drove in their car, and Paul and I rode in ours. We followed one another around town.

During the drive we decided to stop at a few places that are important to us. First, we drove through downtown Pikeville, where Dad used to buy us funnel cakes during Hillbilly Days, which I promise is an actual thing.

During Hillbilly Days, everyone dresses in overalls and puts corncob pipes in their mouths. There is a parade of tired cars sporting wild signs and dragging cans attached to strings behind them. You can hear fantastic bluegrass music, filled with the sounds of banjos and deep country accents. People get on rickety carnival rides and wear straw hats while eating fried everything, sweat dripping down their temples and onto their cheeks.

It's Appalachian glory.

We continued weaving through downtown and passed Hardee's. Most Saturday mornings Dad left money on his low, worn-out coffee table so Jenna and I could grab breakfast there while he slept in. I always ordered biscuits and gravy.

We passed the street where Dad had lived after our parents' divorce, where we had played all those weekends and summers while visiting him. I was surprised to find that the house was no longer standing and nothing was in its place. But I could still see it in my mind's eye.

I recalled him sunbathing on his long plastic beach chair (hours from the beach), wearing rolled up shorts and little black eye covers that people usually use in tanning beds. It was there behind that house when we were middle schoolers that Jenna and I smoked cigarettes we had stolen from Dad. It was awful and cool at the same time.

Dad always smelled like a combination of cologne, aftershave, and Marlboro reds.

We probably played made-up imaginary games like "runaway teenagers" on the same afternoon. Dad had a room full of boxes that were piled up like towers. We would put on the rattiest clothes we could find then hide behind the boxes and pretend to be running away.

Running away from what? I'm not quite sure.

We had driven several miles past where that divorce-house had been when I chuckled to myself about my first French kiss in the parking lot next door. There was a business there, and the neighborhood kids were playing hide and seek. I found myself standing face-to-face with Eric, whom I had known since I was born. We were about twelve at this time, and on that sizzling concrete, in the sweltering summer sun, he gave me the sloppiest kiss of my life.

I vowed never to kiss anyone again.

We continued on past the pool that we had jumped into on humid summer days and the track where we had walked while Dad ran on humid summer nights. Like when he tanned, Dad preferred to wear tiny—embarrassingly tiny—athletic shorts when he ran on the track.

And then there it was, Cowpen Road. The road where Jenna and I grew up, the road that led to the married-house when our parents were still together. Cowpen often flooded if the creek rose too quickly.

Jenna takes after Dad in the "live *BIG*" league. She entered the world during the flood in Pikeville of 1984. Dad had to drive Mom through the floodwater to the top of a hill off of Cowpen Road so that she could be helicoptered to the local hospital—the same hospital Dad would die in thirty-three years later.

It took so long to get to the top of the hill that Jenna was almost delivered in the helicopter.

Dad and Mom appropriately named her Jennifer, which means "white wave." Her name initiated her into Dad's "live *BIG*" legacy.

Dad loved to tell the story.

We had trouble finding the spot where the married-house had been. It, too, had been torn down. It was strange and difficult, but somewhat fitting, to discover the only houses we had lived in with Dad were also gone.

Finally, we saw the familiar little stone bridge that we had used to cross the creek many times in our family's red conversion van. We used our phones to take photos of the land, the creek, the bridge, and the hillside, which was covered in a dense web of trees.

Memories like the cascading waters of 1984 flooded our minds.

Once, Jenna's beloved doll fell into the creek. Dad ran along the creek bank until he caught up to it. Dad leaped into the water after it and saved the day. His large stature always made him heroic to us.

Sometimes when he arrived home from work we would sit on his feet, me on the right and Jenna on the left. Taking large steps, he would walk around the house as we laughed wildly. In my mind we were riding galloping horses across the western plains.

He often had little gifts in the breast pockets of his suit jackets, and, upon returning from work, he would bend down and let us retrieve them as our eyes sparkled with wonder and delight.

We recalled the nights there at this little house too, when we shared bunk beds and Dad sang to Jenna, "On my pillow is a key, to a land of mystery. There are wonders I can see, when I close my eyes." Even as a little girl she had trouble sleeping.

Chapter 3

We knew we did not want to forget how Dad's voice sounded. We also knew we needed food. We had not eaten since lunch the day before. It was immediately apparent where we needed to go: Peking.

Peking is a little Chinese restaurant tucked into a strip mall with bland concrete walls.

For several years after our parents' divorce Jenna and I visited Dad every other Friday night for the weekend. Mom drove us forty-five minutes to the rest area near Natural Bridge after school. Dad, usually late, would meet us in the parking lot, and we would switch to his car. We piled our stuff into Dad's backseat and would drive another hour and forty-five minutes.

After Immanuel Baptist Church, where we were baptized, Peking was one of the first places we'd see upon arriving into Pikeville. Whenever we rounded the corner and saw Peking's green and gold sign lit up, we started salivating.

We grew up on church and Chinese food.

After a long day at school and a two-and-a-half-hour drive, we were ready to enjoy the delights of Peking—sweet and sour chicken, beef and broccoli, and of course those little sugar crusted donuts.

We walked into the restaurant and I was both astounded and grateful to find it just as we had left it years before. The tables were arranged in the way I remembered, and the chairs and decorations had not changed. The buffet had all of its delights in the right places: The ice cream machine was on the far wall, the egg drop soup was on the end, and the egg rolls were piled up in the silver pan in the middle. I needed at least two egg rolls.

Tears streamed down my face at the sight. It was all there to welcome me as it always had.

Don't get me wrong. Novelty is magic; life needs change sometimes. But life—with its deaths interspersed—also desperately needs some things to stay the same.

You need places like Mamaw's house, where the trinkets never get moved and the fifty-year-old toys stick around. When life smacks you in the face like a cold blast of New England winter wind, you need familiarity, something you can count on to keep your heart warm so as not to become callous. I needed this particular salty, fat-saturated Americanized Chinese food with *these* gold and green decorations in *this* strip mall. On this day it was sameness that I found magical.

I cried all the way through the meal. I cried as we sat down at the table where we usually sat on Friday nights. It was a few hours early, but it was a Friday. I cried as I selected food from the buffet. I cried while I ate. I cried as our husbands paid the lunch bill, and I cried during the walk back to our car in the parking lot.

I cried as we drove away, wondering if I would ever be back again, since Pikeville is so far from where I live. Other than nostalgia, I knew then that from that day forward I would have no reason to return.

That evening I found myself in a fetal position on the floor of Jenna's spare bedroom. There is a space between the wall and the bed—roughly three feet—and there I was curled up on the carpet clutching my father's shirt and his pajama pants, weeping uncontrollably.

I do not even know how I got there. I must have just collapsed from the pain of those four weeks, from the overwhelming sorrow of the previous twenty-four hours. At some point I looked up and through my tears saw Paul sitting on the bed right above me.

"Grief is a lonely, empty room. I'm sitting outside the door holding vigil."

Paul was indeed holding vigil for me. He could not open the door. My grief was different than his. He could not do anything to lessen the ache in my bleeding heart. But there he sat, a witness to my agony. He stayed near.

It is incredibly difficult to lovingly bear witness to grief rather than walking away or trying to fix it. It is much harder to share space with grief, to breathe its pungent air.

4

Unleashed

I cry aloud to God,
aloud to God, that God may hear me.
In the day of my trouble I seek the Lord;
in the night my hand is stretched out
without wearying;
my soul refuses to be comforted.
I think of God, and I moan;
I meditate, and my spirit faints.
You keep my eyelids from closing;
I am so troubled that I cannot speak.

—Psalm 77:1–4

In the months that followed those four weeks of hell, Job became a biblical character I could relate to. I can imagine him. Covered in ash, dark circles under his eyes from too little sleep and too much pain.

He loses all but one of his family members and everything he owns, even his dignity.

At the end of himself, Job wants to talk to God.

When Job reaches out for compassion, wanting God to explain why everything has gone so wrong, God says a lot of different things, but one line has always stuck with me. At one point God asks Job if he knows when the mountain goats give birth.

"Um, no. No, I don't know when. Thanks, God."

Roll eyes. Shrug shoulders. Go back to crying.

For over a year and a half, I would feel as I imagined Job felt. It seemed God was going on about goats while I was praying about my pain.

I love Job's story because it is authentic and difficult to understand. It has been debated for centuries. It demonstrates so well how quickly bad theology emerges when people are hurting and life is unbearable.

During those months, I felt connected with the prophet Elijah as well, as if I too had traveled through my own kind of wilderness and entered a cave. Daily, I was hoping to walk out of my emptiness and experience God's presence in magnificent, obvious ways—as a whirlwind, an earthquake, a fire.

Instead, I met the God of unknowing, of descent, of sheer silence.

Study joy? Unthinkable. Laughable even. So disturbing a prospect that I almost vowed to be anything but joyful.

I had read everything I could get my hands on about joy for the first months after arriving at Yale.

Now the word made me cringe.

What a lie.

Life was not joyful.

It was a long walk toward death.

Grief was every meal—breakfast, lunch, and dinner. It was an all-I-could-eat buffet.

It seemed the sorrow of death nursed every other sorrow I had ever felt—for the separations between family members, for words left unsaid and actions left undone, for the last decade of Dad's life, for other things I cannot bear to type.

Sorrow is fertile ground for the blooms of other sorrows.

Attending church felt impossible for multiple Sundays after my family's four weeks of hell. So I ended up staying at home and crying for two to three hours instead. Sometimes I journaled during these hours, but not often because it did not seem to help.

I talked to God every once in a while. Our chats usually involved me asking God why life is so heartbreaking. Occasionally I took long walks and cried all over the city.

Sometimes I was on my knees, face buried in the couch, crying. Other times I just sat crying while staring at the living room wall. Many Sundays I baked muffins and cried all over them while mixing the batter and putting it into the tins.

I wondered whether Paul could taste my tears in them.

Grief is messy. It is runny-nose, tear-stained-cheeks, cry-in-a-ball-on-the-floor, can't-get-out-of-your-pajamas-till-noon, eat-and-drink-to-fill-the-soul-with-something-other-than-sadness, feel-like-you're-going-to-die-of-a-broken-heart messy.

When your heart is broken you feel like the walking dead. I screamed, lifted heavy weights at the gym, took long walks in the cold just to feel something. Anything was better than feeling dead too.

Yet there were also those days when I wanted to try and ignore that I was grieving. So I did anything possible to not focus on the fact that people I love are gone. On days like that I dressed up and went to work like a normal person who does not spend her Sundays crying into muffins.

One day that I can distinctly remember, I went into a work

meeting I was leading and presented myself as organized and put-together as possible, exactly how I wanted to be seen. I tried to appear confident, focused, emotionless. And then out of nowhere someone said something that brought everything back. Everyone began talking casually about preventing suicide and the "issues" around it.

Before I could stop myself or sneak away to a bathroom, I was crying and talking loudly over everyone, explaining that one of my family members died by suicide last December, and it was too painful to hear them all talk about it in a work meeting like that.

And then everyone looked at me with *those eyes*.

The kind of eyes that make you feel like you just stepped outside of the shower dripping wet and someone walked in to find you exposed, naked. Immediately, I felt embarrassed because they knew more than I wanted them to know, they got to see something they didn't deserve to see—my most tender, vulnerable self.

If you Google "crying at work," numerous articles about managing your tears will be offered to you. No one wants to cry in front of other people, especially at work. Crying is seen as unprofessional and awkward. If you are crying, it means you cannot control yourself.

We have been socially trained to feel ashamed, disempowered, and regretful after crying in public spaces.

Babies cry, not adults. That's why we say it is important not to cry over spilled milk. Crying is improperly viewed as weakness, vulnerability, neediness—all of which are completely human and somehow also entirely unacceptable in most settings.

Crying makes people uncomfortable, including the person who is crying.

When I lead a class or workshop and tell people, "This is a space where you can be vulnerable, where you can cry if you need to," people still apologize when they cry. Tears are usually followed with some sort of defense: "I'm not usually this emotional," "I don't know why I am crying," or "I need to pull it together."

We even have a phrase for crying that is perceived as particularly unwelcomed, the "ugly cry." As if fully demonstrating sorrow is unattractive rather than good and beautiful.

Sometimes I'd get home from being my put-together work-self and give anything to feel near my dad again. So I'd go to my closet and find Dad's blanket. The one that was on him the day he died. It's in a plastic baggie.

I'd hope his smell was still there even though it had been months.

I would pick up his hat and think of how ridiculous it looked but just wish so badly he could be there to put it on. I often got out pictures of a day in elementary school when he took me hiking—the ones where we were both making silly faces.

I would weep, hard, for that little girl who loved him so.

Other days I looked at photos of Mason and Dustin on social media and on my laptop, from days when they were smiling without a care in the world. And suddenly I'd be back in the kitchen listening to the song from the drive to Kentucky on repeat—the one from Dustin's funeral—and baking more tear-filled muffins.

The cycles of tears repeated:

Cry for Dustin's young kids. Cry for my cousin and my sister and other family members and friends who loved Dustin, Mason, and Dad. Cry for self. Cry because suicide is overwhelming and devastating. Cry because my nephew was thriving and just starting his life as an adult. Cry because opioids destroyed Dad's life. Cry because three family members died in four weeks.

Get dressed. Go to work. Make it a few hours, sometimes a few days. Repeat.

Grief felt like a cloud was over me everywhere I went. But not like the cloud that represented God's presence and guided the Israelites, not the good kind. This cloud literally made the world gloomy all of the time.

Even the most brilliant colors were dismal. Even the sounds of children laughing did not reach my ears.

Grief made everything that was terrible even more terrible. The wind felt colder against my bare hands. People who did not keep their word or neglected to say hello to me suddenly seemed like enemies.

Kids screaming in Target (probably because, like me, they

wanted to leave without spending their life savings) were far less tolerable. The store clerk who wanted to know (again) if I was looking for something in particular might as well have been asking for a piggyback ride.

Grief is a pile of dirty laundry. You sift through stained pants just to find soiled shirts. And each one carries a memory. You have to carefully examine every piece, every remembrance. You can leave the pile on the floor for as long as you want, but to actually deal with it you must eventually touch it all.

It is the harshest reality.

Grief is the moment when you walk into your home, welcome the embrace of another person, sit somewhere familiar, and you suddenly realize that you cannot be physically near your loved ones anymore.

If you're lucky you might be able to hear their voice on a voicemail or in a video, but not in person. You can cry as much as you want and be willing to pay any price, but you cannot feel their skin against yours. You cannot share the same space in the ways you once did.

On its cruelest days, grief feels like an assailant who waits around the corner in order to cover your mouth from behind. It surprises you unexpectedly, takes your breath, terrorizes you, and reminds you that life will never be the same.

It is hard to depict grief adequately.

Interestingly, grief and joy are similar in their inexpressibility. I describe grief and think, "No, it's worse than that." I describe joy and understand it is far more marvelous.

It's as if the moment I articulate a definition of grief or joy, I diminish them.

At least with Dustin and Dad, there seemed to be things I could blame—depression and anxiety mostly—reasons for their deaths that did not bring comfort but were reasons nonetheless. My nephew's death was different, though.

Chapter 4

He was merely twenty-two years old. He was blooming. He enjoyed his work and had good friends. He was on a great track, seemingly enjoying life, talking to his mom weekly, paying his own bills, taking care of himself.

The longer I contemplated his death, the more senseless it felt. There was no need for him to die so early. What was the point? Why was his life finished when there was still so much life to be lived?

Stef's grief was palpable. She was so vulnerable and honest about the ways his death upended her life, not just with me and my other sisters but also in her social media posts. She was willing to express in a raw, genuine way how the grief of losing her first child, her dearest boy, had transformed everything.

Mason's death changed the way she saw everyone around her, changed how she related to God, changed how she oriented herself to every day and to every task. Stef has allowed his death to soften her spirit (even more than it already was).

Grief has made her gentler and more loving and more attuned to others' pain. It seems grief can consume us and make us bitter or—if we choose, like Stef, to openly acknowledge grief and fully express it—mysteriously grief can develop us into more present, more human, more compassionate beings.

She sees Mason all around her. She senses his presence in each new venture she takes up and in every moment she breathes, as if her breath sustains both her life and his, as only a mother can do.

In the midst of my family's sorrow, I was strangely comforted by the fact that the word "wept" is used numerous times throughout the Bible. Right off the bat, many of Genesis's main characters weep: Hagar, Esau, Jacob, Joseph, Benjamin, and the rest of Joseph's brothers.

Throughout the Hebrew Scriptures the Israelites weep again and again. And there are others still—Job, Orpah and Ruth, Hannah, David, Jeremiah, King Joash, Hezekiah, and Nehemiah.

When we get to the New Testament, its most prominent figures also weep, sometimes uncontrollably: Mary, Peter, and Jesus.

I am especially drawn to Mary's story of grief.

Mary and her sister Martha were upset because Lazarus, their brother, was sick. They sent word to Jesus asking him to come quickly. It makes sense that Mary and Martha trusted Jesus to come as quickly as possible and perform one of his miracles for Lazarus because Jesus was close to Lazarus. Jesus performed miracles all the time.

Here's the thing: Jesus heard the news of Lazarus's sickness and then stayed where he was two more days.

Two more days.

People have shared reasons why Jesus had to wait. But the point is that by the time Jesus arrived, mourners were all around Mary and Martha. Lazarus was dead and was actually already in a tomb.

When Jesus finally reached their town, Martha went out to meet him but Mary stayed home.

I see you, Mary; I am picking up what you are putting down. I probably would have stayed home, too.

Eventually, at her sister's urging, she went to see Jesus. She wept at his feet.

Interestingly, when *both* Martha and Mary saw Jesus, even though this happens at different times and in different places, they bluntly told him the same thing: "Lord, if you had been here, my brother would not have died."

I have been there, too. "God, if only you had done so and so, what is would not be."

After Mary said this, she was distraught, perhaps resentful. Mary cried so much that she needed to be consoled by the mourners who surrounded her. And then Jesus became visibly disturbed. Jesus looked at Lazarus's tomb, Mary, and the mourners around her weeping, and he cried too.

Jesus wept.

It is the shortest and mightiest sentence in the Bible.

Why did Jesus weep?

As playwright Oscar Wilde put it: "I have said that behind sorrow there is always sorrow. It were wiser still to say that behind sorrow there is always a soul."

One day fear moved into my heart. It did not just pitch a tent for a few nights. It rented an Airbnb for months.

I became terrified of death.

To be honest, I had not thought that much about death before those four weeks of hell. Seemingly out of the blue I began to think of death daily. I found myself imagining everyone I love dying. I saved every voicemail.

I still do.

Just in case the person dies, I want to be sure I will still be able to hear their voice. I feel similarly about cards. I hoard cards and letters. I want to make sure that if someone I love passes away, I can look at their words and easily remember our connection.

A few months after Dad died, Paul went to the Postal Service drop box a couple of blocks from our house and I realized how fearful I had actually become. He said he was going to walk to the drop box and put in a letter. I was at home writing, and so I was lost in my own thoughts for quite a while. About forty-five minutes later I realized he had not returned, and I tried to call him. It was a mere ten-minute walk, so I wondered where he was. He did not answer. I called him two more times about ten minutes later, only to walk around the house and discover he had left his phone behind.

I began to panic.

"Where you take greatest joy you will also have the greatest fear."

My heart raced. I got in our shared car and began driving around the neighborhood. I looked up and down multiple streets. I drove our usual walking loop, imagining that he had decided to extend the walk since it was an unusually nice New England day.

I could not find him anywhere.

Abruptly, my panic manifested in irrepressible tears. I drove home to see if he had returned. He had not. So I drove other streets, streets where it made no sense for him to walk but that were within walking distance. I returned home in a terrified, grief-stricken state.

He was still not back.

At that point it had been about two hours. From our couch, I googled "when to call 911 after someone has gone missing." I decided I was going to call when it had been three hours. I fixated on the unimaginable. What if I never saw him again? What if I never knew what happened to him? How would I live without him?

While reflecting on these horrifying questions and intensely crying, I heard Paul open the front door and come up the stairs. He was immediately worried about me when he saw my face. "What happened?" he asked.

"I thought you were dead."

He felt terrible and tried to comfort me, explaining that he had been talking to Cedric. Cedric is the piano player at the church that was down the street from the house where we lived, and the drop box is across the street from the church. Paul saw Cedric's car in the parking lot and decided to go in and chat with him.

Their chat turned into a meaningful two-and-a-half-hour conversation—fantastic for Paul and Cedric, mental torture for me.

I shared this story only with a couple of people. Even still, other than Paul and eventually my therapist, I don't think anyone knew that I was walking around terrified of death.

I guess it starts when we are young.

Most of us remember the chant from middle school, "Don't be a scaredy-cat." Fear should not be expressed and discussed; it should be overcome (as quickly as possible). Many people are encouraged throughout their lives to be the opposite of sensitive. To be tough instead. Fear, like crying, is perceived as weakness.

Men who are "real men" don't cry and are, of course, never afraid. Men who talk about their emotions, especially fear, are viewed as poorly adjusted.

Too many people are taught to bury emotions rather than give words to them. Most of us have never been asked to name our fears and reflect on why certain things scare us. We have not been told that it is understandable that we are afraid sometimes. Maybe that is why I never thought about discussing my newfound fear with other people.

After teaching and being taught to hide emotions again and again, we should not be surprised when we hear people—or perhaps ourselves—say, "I feel nothing."

The philosopher Seneca would have offered me an alternative to living in isolated fear, one that is as unhelpful as repressing it: "You will cease to fear, if you cease to hope."

In other words, hope makes you vulnerable to fear. Hope means you have expectations, you have your eyes on a horizon, you are waiting on something or someone. It means you are imagining things will work out, things will be different. Hope requires some sort of optimism.

Seneca understood that hope then makes you susceptible to fearfulness.

What if things don't work out the way you want them to? What if you hope something will come but it does not? What if things never work out? What if they never change? If you don't want to live with these kinds of questions, simply stop hoping and you will stop fearing.

It might seem Seneca was on to something.

Yet, what Seneca did not seem to understand is that hope is "the anticipation of joy." Without hope, we also become closed to joy.

Hope and joy keep despair at bay.

———

There was a package on the front porch. Upon returning home from work, Paul asked me why I had not brought it inside.

Immediately I was enraged.

He had asked me that morning to bring in a package if I saw it on the porch, but from my point of view the evening had been too busy for such meaningless tasks.

Defending myself—which I am great at, by the way—I told Paul that I had just had a really important conversation with my sisters. We had arranged a Google Hangout conversation and ended up talking together about Dad for the first time in a long time.

Basically, I wanted and desperately needed time in between the conversation I had with my sisters about Dad and the discussion about the package on the porch, but instead of asking for time, I yelled louder to drive home the point that what I had been doing was much more significant than a package on the porch.

Paul stayed calm, but he wanted to try and talk about what had happened. He wanted to understand why I did not think our conversation earlier that day (the one where he had asked me to get the package from the porch) was important.

I wanted to understand why he did not think my conversation with my sisters was more important than that conversation and the package. We found ourselves at an impasse.

But it was not just any impasse. In my mind, Paul had somehow forgotten that my dad was dead.

He was neglecting my grief. Rather than taking some time to cool off and come back together to figure out how we could talk through these things, I lashed out at him, screaming, about— well, just as with the moment on the pavement with the cell phone after learning about Dustin's suicide, everything about this other moment is blurry.

But I can remember screaming at the top of my lungs, so loudly that for weeks I was embarrassed to even imagine what the people on the second floor of our rented house thought of me.

It was as if the living room went dark and I was just letting loose on the universe. I had wanted to yell at someone for a long time. Perhaps I hoped my own screaming could compensate for what had felt like the sheer silence of everyone around me.

During those months following the deaths of my family members, I had felt misunderstood again and again. I found myself walking around angrily, thinking, "Why don't you acknowledge the pain that I am in?"

Several months after my weeks of hell, I woke up to discover that before I had even gotten out of bed, I was already angry. I would unexpectedly realize I was fuming in grocery store lines or while walking down the sidewalk because someone did not say, "Excuse me."

I was angry at death, at depression and addiction, and at how God "works" (which often feels like God has an out-of-office email with no date of return).

I was angry that no one could heal Dustin's depression, or save Mason's life, or cure Dad's addiction. I found myself livid while sitting in traffic and, eventually, during church sermons. I would look at the people leading the worship services and think to myself, "You don't get how life really is."

It felt like I was losing my grip on the faith I had known so clearly all my life. About a year after my weeks of hell we changed churches, but still most Sundays when I sat in the pews it seemed the words of the sermons, songs, and prayers raced past me down the aisle and out the back door.

One day I became aware that I was basically furious at the fact that life was still going on. The sun was still rising and setting. My housing manager still wanted rent on the first of the month. Dishes still needed to be washed. I still had to go to my gynecology appointment.

Everything had changed, and yet nothing had.

And it made me so angry that I wanted to run around town screaming that everyone needed to wake up and pay attention because the world *was* different. It would never be the same. It had become more terrifying and more upsetting.

But I thought better of it because I did not want everyone to realize just how sad, fearful, and angry I truly was. They might have concluded I didn't belong at my Ivy League job, getting paid to teach everyone about joy and the life worth living.

Similar to sadness and fear, we are culturally trained to feel that anger should be suppressed.

People who do not "manage" their emotions are perceived as less intelligent, as people who lack leadership potential.

Even when we grow up in households where people express emotions freely, there is little to no education about how to do this in constructive, healing ways. We have few, if any, rituals for beneficial emotional expression.

We are seldom taught how to be angry (unless we are made to take an anger management course). Instead we are implicitly taught to conceal or ignore our anger—even if it is righteous anger, even if it is anger tied to profound loss—and if we cannot do so, we are judged accordingly.

I know, because I am the one judging people who become extremely angry in public spaces.

Anger, especially, is wrongly categorized as a "bad" emotion. We are pressured to not acknowledge it lest we *give in to it.*

Writer Soraya Chemaly explains: "In the Western world, anger in women has been widely associated with 'madness.'" Angry women are often categorized as hysterical women and thus viewed as untrustworthy and less credible. Exhibited anger in women is also typically considered as unattractive and unfeminine.

It is no wonder why I did not want other people to know about my anger.

Black women have suffered the most from general criticism of anger. There is a pervasive harmful, racist stereotype of the "angry Black woman" in media, which wrongly depicts Black women as overly aggressive, hotheaded, and ill-mannered. Due to this stereotype, Black women especially feel the pressure to carefully suppress their anger so they will not be perceived in a negative way.

Yet anger is a natural, important human emotion that if named, expressed, and worked through can be powerfully constructive. Even Jesus got angry.

At one point he met a man with a shriveled hand in a synagogue. Onlookers watched carefully to see whether Jesus would break the Sabbath law and heal him; they were ready to judge him and to act on those judgments. When Jesus saw the hardness of people's hearts around him, he looked at them *with anger* and grieved.

We should be angered when people around us have no compassion. And we should be allowed to express anger about death that has no mercy. Instead we are shaped to believe emotions should be restricted rather than deeply felt.

Given societal pressure to hide emotions, I tried my best to isolate myself and feel my grief—especially its forms of weeping, fear, and anger—alone. And I looked forward to those moments when I could privately unleash my raw emotions.

During the Package on the Porch Debacle, it began to rain. I walked outside anyway. It was really dark in the town I lived in, and downtown was not the safest place to walk at night. Paul begged me to stay and talk things out with him. He even offered to be the one to leave so I could think at home alone.

But I refused.

I told him that I had to walk alone. As in the months before, I felt as if my only choice was to express my emotions in solitary confinement, so I had to get out of the house. The sky opened and rain poured. I left without an umbrella (on purpose), so my clothes got soaked. I liked that. I wanted to be drenched and cold.

I wanted to *decisively* suffer rather than have suffering happen to me.

I was done with suffering that I had not caused. I wanted to wander the streets alone because I felt alone in my anger, fear, and profound sadness. As I roamed the streets, I thought about how unseen and disconnected from other people I felt. And this made me even more dejected, which made me even angrier.

I embraced the rage.

And since I was by myself, it was an anger I did not have to suppress.

Between the Drop Box Devastation and the Package on the Porch Debacle, I realized I needed help. (And apparently needed to stop using the Postal Service.)

The thing is, I needed a particular kind of help.

I needed *helpful* help.

In the midst of my deep-seated sorrow, fear, and anger, I did not need people to simply tell me that everything was going to be all right.

I definitely did not want to hear that the suffering of my family was or would be part of some divine strategy. I was not looking for tips and tricks on how to find positivity.

What I needed was room to work through my laments: Dustin's children deserve to have their father around to watch them grow up. Mason should have been given the opportunity to get married if he wanted to, to stress over a mortgage, to find his first gray hair. I wish Dad had recovered from addiction and come to my wedding and died with dignity. These are some of my laments, and I needed to grieve them.

I needed healing space to confront the painful realities of life.

Sometimes we are indeed given more than we can handle. Sometimes what we hope for never materializes. Sometimes what does not kill us also does not make us stronger. Sometimes the plan God has for us means we live in exile.

I sought help in several forms—therapy, journaling, meditation, gym workouts, hikes, and in some not so healthy ways—but nothing seemed to promote the healing I longed for.

Not until I walked into a prison Bible study.

5

Helpful Help

Joy is what we feel, and as self-reflective beings know we feel, in situations, real or imaginary, in which what was lost is found; what was missing restored; what constrained is lifted; what we desire arrives; or what arrives satisfies a desire we hadn't known we'd had.

—Adam Potkay, *The Story of Joy*

"What is your deepest longing?"
"Damn."

That's what the corrections officer said as we walked to the lobby of the prison. He was my escort back to the prison's front entrance from the room where I met with the women for Bible study.

"What would you say? What is your deepest longing on this night, January 16, 2019?"

He shrugged his shoulders and was clearly uncomfortable, but he was tuned into the conversation.

"I have no idea. I have no idea how to answer that question," he said.

I had asked the same question to the women who attended Bible study that evening, and they had plenty to say. These women knew what was worth wanting. Their responses were articulate and powerful.

They longed to be reunited with their children.

They wanted to give and receive forgiveness. "I just want the strength to move forward and forgive myself," Amy said over and over again throughout the night. Amy had been addicted to various drugs and living on the streets since she was a teenager. She was still young, in her early twenties. Her mom had been addicted to pills while she was growing up.

Like my dad, her mom often became drowsy from the pills and fell asleep with a cigarette in her hand.

Amy smoked crack for the first time with her mom when she was just fourteen years old. Shortly after, when she was a sophomore in high school, her mom encouraged her to get a job to help support the household. Amy's mom signed paperwork to ensure she was released from the school system.

Not long after, Amy began selling her body to pay bills and to support her own addictions. In a way similar to her mom, Amy found herself bound to substances.

Cycles of addiction are potent.

These women wanted sobriety, jobs, homes to call their own. Several women longed for good health. Lee had been told there was a lump in her breast just two days earlier. She longed for it to be benign.

Tonya longed for heaven. She said, "Take me right now. I can't wait to get there." We learned later in the evening that her beautiful blonde hair had been falling out in clumps and she did not know why. She wondered if it was the stress of being in prison.

Then Ms. Aaliyah jumped in.

There were a few older women in the group, women in their fifties and sixties. Everyone used the term "Ms." to address them as a way of showing them respect. The other Bible study leaders and I followed suit.

Ms. Aaliyah said she wanted God to remove the hate in her heart.

I was immediately uncomfortable with her longing.

Was it that I was appalled by her confession of hatred, or, more likely, was it that I could not imagine admitting such a longing in front of a crowd?

Charlotte, in the prison for murder, said she longed for discernment from the Holy Spirit. She wanted to respond to the Spirit's voice and not to the voices of others who might try to sway her from God's path for her.

In prison, I learned not to assume much about people—not to assume that people convicted of murder don't long to hear God's voice as much as I do.

When you practice faithful presence week in and week out in a circle without technology or any other resource for hours at a time, you learn to ask questions and listen patiently. You learn about true seeing.

You learn to pay attention to people's faces, to the way they squint their eyes when they are trying to make sense of life's darkest hours. You learn to look with compassion at the way their feet sway back and forth and their fingers nervously grip their jeans as they tell their stories. And you learn about the relationship between violence and pain.

You learn to read people's lives like you read poetry.

If you allow it, reading people's lives will teach you empathy—for your coworkers, for your family members, for the grocery store clerk, for your neighbor who does not mow their lawn enough, and for the stranger on the street who's doped up and asking for money, again.

Twelve months of faithful presence in a barren room in a prison taught me about humility and honesty too.

Not humble-bragging. Humility.

And not partial honesty. Real honesty, which is all or nothing.

Nothing is half-baked in prison. That is why I felt so alive there.

A year after my family's weeks of hell, while still overwhelmed by grief, I filled out paperwork to join a team from my church that leads the Bible study at this prison.

It makes very little sense that I did this. I was stressed about my job. I was working roughly sixty hours a week. And as I described, my sorrow had turned into extreme fear and anger.

But God had been nudging me toward prison ministry for several years, and on one particular evening at church I suddenly surrendered to this invitation.

I had no way of knowing then that this act of surrender was all that God needed, that the prison ministry I signed up for was going to minister to me.

One Sunday, people who had been going to the prison hung prayer requests from the women who were a part of the Bible study on a Christmas tree in the sanctuary. I took a few off the tree, brought them home, read them over the next few days, and prayed for them.

I was moved by the women's truthfulness, and I was sobered by the depth of their pain. Their emotions were so clearly articulated. They wanted to share what they were feeling with other people. Unlike me, they were willing to express complex emotions in community.

Subconsciously, I wanted to surround myself with companions like these women. I desperately needed other people around me who were willing to be candid about their deepest needs, confusions, and struggles. I no longer wanted to be alone in my sorrow, fear, and anger.

During orientation, I realized I would need to gain a new understanding of myself at the prison.

We could not take anything into the prison with us—not our cell phones, our keys, or our IDs. We could not tell the women who were incarcerated anything about ourselves, not where we worked or lived, not our last names, not information about our families. We were told in orientation this was because the women were "great manipulators," people who would deceive us and take advantage of us if given the chance.

Before heading to the prison, we had to call to make sure it was not on lockdown. Lockdown happens when there is a medical emergency, an item goes missing, or a fight breaks out, among other possibilities. When lockdown occurs, no one can leave or enter the prison. Every person who is incarcerated has to be counted, and until the "event" is resolved no one can leave her cell.

Sometimes lockdown happens and the women can't move around in the prison for multiple days in a row.

Upon arrival at the prison, our Bible study team members walk into the lobby from the parking lot and stand in line with our licenses. Our team is made up of men and women of various ethnicities and ages.

It is important for the women who attend the Bible study (who represent various ethnicities and ages themselves) to see diversity in our leadership. I think our diversity helps the women to see themselves in us, to believe they can lead too, no matter their age or ethnicity, and to see what it looks like to collaborate with and become a community with all sorts of people. Plus, for some of the women the men on the team represent a totally new view of masculinity, men who do not abuse them or want sex from them or see them as less than themselves.

We pass each license through a small hole in a dark plexiglass window to a corrections officer, who passes it back to another corrections officer, who then looks up each one of us in a computer.

Since we are in the system and approved, our names are written down in black pen in a notebook along with the time we arrived. One of the corrections officers hands each of us a prison badge in exchange for our IDs.

I always go to the bathroom right after the exchange because I know it is my last opportunity for two hours.

We take off our shoes and anything that might make the metal detector go off. We put a quarter into the slot of one of the lockers, place our keys and cell phones inside, turn the locker key, and take it with us.

Once the escort arrives to take us inside the prison we walk through the metal detector. If there are no buzzes, we put everything back on and they open the first locked door so that we can show the officers everything we have with us.

The officers flip through our Bibles and loose-leaf paper. We cannot bring paper for the women unless it is approved. We cannot have staples or paper clips on our papers because they could be used by the women to hurt others or themselves.

Everything about prison prepares you for impending doom.

Other than Bibles and paper, we normally just have two pens and a sign-up sheet with us. If the search goes well, a second door opens to a small holding space where there are four doors: the one we just walked through behind us; one to the left for visitors; one to the right, which seems to be for offices; and one in front of us. We stand in the holding space looking at the white doors and the white walls until the door in front of us magically opens.

This holding space and its stark whiteness are reminiscent of a mental health hospital ward—sterile, controlled, unnerving.

A group of officers watches from behind glass. They open these doors. We cannot see them, but they can see us. They are the same officers watching the security cameras all over the prison.

When visiting a prison, you get a tiny sense of how an inmate feels.

You get a badge with a number in exchange for an identification card with your name and personal details. You are viewed with suspicion and questioned. People are constantly making sure you are not doing something wrong or bringing in what is considered contraband. You are escorted everywhere you go. You are watched closely.

At this point in the all-white holding space, we are only thirty feet from the parking lot and we have already walked through three locked doors. We move past women on our left who are waiting on a bench to see their visitors.

Each time they see a visitor, the women walk through a metal detector on their way to and on their way from the visit. The women sit across the table from their visitors. About three feet separate them. They can hug if they can reach each other, but there should be no lingering hugs.

We then walk past the area that is likely the most demoralizing, a door marked "Strip Search Area."

The women are strip-searched upon arrival at the prison, after visits, and after court dates. They remove all of their clothes and undergarments, bend over, spread their buttocks, and cough in front of corrections officers—male and female.

Most of the officers at this prison are men.

Most of the women in prison in the United States have been sexually or physically abused by a man, some by many men, during their lives.

One night during Bible study, a woman shared about being constantly beat up by her boyfriend. I gently asked the women in the Bible study if they had similar experiences they wanted to talk about. Every woman present had been physically abused, sexually abused, or both—by family members, partners, or both.

I walk by the strip search area and wonder how strip searches could possibly aid in these women's restoration.

If a prison's aim is to dehumanize, we cannot expect people to come out more connected to other people's (and their own) humanity, more in touch with their emotions, more loving, more whole.

And without these capacities, how will they be healed and stop harming themselves and others?

The escort takes us to another door, also locked, and opens it for us. We walk down a long hallway with white concrete walls and concrete floors to yet another locked door. Finally, we begin making our way outside to the building with the Bible study. It's the equivalent of one long city block. The sidewalk has two sides with a yellow line marking their separation. The women in prison are supposed to walk on one side and volunteers, staff, and officers on the other.

Everything in prison is about making people who are incarcerated feel as diminished and insignificant as possible. As most people know, when someone goes to prison, they are given a number and a badge to wear that displays this number and the date they arrived.

They are no longer called by their first names and are often associated with these numbers.

The number helps reveal how long a person has been in prison because similar numbers were given out in similar years. The longer a person has been in prison, likely, the worse his or her crime is. Ms. Aaliyah has been in prison over fifteen years; her badge reveals this truth. Her number is unlike any other woman's number, much shorter because she has been there so long. Whenever other women realize she has been there fifteen years, they gasp.

In prison, you are your sins.

We know what happens to people in the Bible whose entire identity becomes equated with the worst thing they have ever done; it causes death. Sometimes it is a kind of death that destroys someone else as in the case of David. Other times it is the kind of death that extinguishes one's own light as in the case of Judas.

We make our way down the winding sidewalk with the yellow line and are escorted to a building where the women live. The escort asks the corrections officers watching over both sides of the building to call "Protestant Bible study" over the loudspeaker.

Sometimes the officers actually do this for both sides and every floor of the building, and sometimes they do not. It seems to depend on how the officers sitting there are feeling. Numerous times, I went to Bible study and heard from women that they were not present the week before because the officers never called it on their floor. Sometimes officers would neglect an entire side of the building.

When we would notice on the sign-up sheet that women were not present from one side of the building, we would try to talk to the officers, but they would wave us off, explaining they *had* called it but no one wanted to come.

Before heading back to the front of the prison, the escort unlocks the two doors that lead into the room where we hold Bible study and brings us a body alarm to wear. We attach it to a beltloop on our jeans. We are supposed to press the button on it during an emergency. We were told during orientation that this could be especially helpful if taken hostage.

Like I said, impending doom.

We finally enter the round room. It has about thirty small, blue plastic chairs, a couple of paperback Bibles, a stack of tattered yoga mats (which I am not sure ever get used), and two rectangular, brown tables.

We push the tables against the walls and arrange the chairs so that they make the biggest circle possible and put the sign-up sheet on one of the tables. The women have to write down their name, their badge number, and on which side of the building they live.

A few minutes after arriving, the women file into the room. They are all wearing the same T-shirt and jeans, and on cold nights the same sweatshirt, unless they have ever tried to escape the prison.

Those women are in bright yellow scrubs.

I am not sure how long they have to wear the scrubs after trying to escape. One woman wore them for months to Bible study. I never asked her about what happened. It was quite an event when she eventually walked in wearing the standard T-shirt and jeans.

After they arrive, we enthusiastically welcome the women with our voices because we are unable to greet them in any other way. Supportive actions are managed in prison too. At this particular prison, women who are incarcerated are not supposed to touch one another, and no volunteer or prison worker is supposed to ever touch them either, which may seem like a good policy until you realize that means no hugs, no pats on the back, and no handshakes, ever.

Even if someone you love dies while you are in this prison, you cannot go to their funeral, and no one is supposed to comfort you with any kind of touch. You can be alone in a room with their dead body or ashes for thirty minutes with two officers watching, but that is it. It does not matter if it is your child, your spouse, your sibling or your parent.

And this same rule applies to everyone at this prison, whether there because their body was trafficked for sex, because they had an addiction, or because they were found sleeping in an abandoned building that said, "No trespassing," as in Amy's case.

If you are in prison for a few months and no one is visiting you, a lack of touch may not be entirely damaging to your soul. But if you are there for fifteen years, like Ms. Aaliyah has been, a lack of touch can minimize your humanity so much that you cannot imagine leaving prison.

Ms. Aaliyah cannot imagine leaving.

If there is an existence for Ms. Aaliyah outside the barbed wire fence, she cannot see it. At one point, she struggled so much with the idea of leaving that she blatantly did things she knew she should not do to get more time in prison.

During my first month of visits to the prison, I learned that our team primarily served the women in the mental health ward and the women on suicide watch. I also learned that the majority of the women in the Bible study were serving time because of addictions to heroin or crack cocaine.

Shockingly, "today, there are more people behind bars for a drug offense than the number of people who were in prison or jail for *any* crime in 1980." Approximately half of the people in prisons and jails are dependent on a substance when they enter the system.

Many of the women who are incarcerated for drug-related charges are poor mothers, and so mass incarceration and America's opioid crisis are together significantly affecting America's children. In fact, *80 percent* of women who are incarcerated in the United States are mothers, *the majority* of whom are serving time in prisons for abusing or trafficking drugs—usually heroin, crack, or both.

Prison has violent, detrimental effects on these mothers' lives and the lives of their children.

It is difficult to determine exactly how much higher the likelihood of a child ending up in prison becomes after a parent is incarcerated. One study I found determined a child is three times more likely to become involved in the justice system if they have a parent in prison. In any case, being incarcerated aggravates mental health issues, puts people at a greater risk of suicide, and increases the likelihood that people will become financially unstable and homeless, all of which affect the lives of their children.

The building the Bible study team serves is largely a mental hospital and sober house.

I remember thinking how remarkable it was that after everything my family had gone through I was regularly talking with and learning from women who deal with significant mental distress, addictions, and suicidal thoughts.

Over the months, I realized they were helping me understand Dad's and Dustin's pain.

In prison, my research on joy, my faith (and doubt), and my four weeks of hell collided.

One night the women were sitting at a table and drawing on a piece of blank paper with markers I had brought.

I had asked for special permission to bring both items to the Bible study that night. I had to count every marker and make sure every marker that I brought in was taken out. I also had to make sure that no one took any extra blank sheets of paper back to their room (that would have been a gift, and no gifts are allowed) and to make sure that I did not take any drawing home with me (that would have been accepting something from a woman who was incarcerated—also not allowed).

Around the table, as they drew, I overheard the women trying to help one another figure out what to do after prison, where to sleep and how to stay off drugs when denied a program for recovery.

Hailey was especially worried about this.

She was thinking she would be released right after her upcoming court date. If indeed she was, she had no idea what to do after walking out of the courthouse. She had no place to go, no one she felt she could call who was not addicted to drugs, and no money. She had tried to get a bed at a sober house but had not yet been granted one.

The women at the table told Hailey that if she could not connect with help before leaving prison, she should get on a train at the station near the courthouse. They explained that she should take the train to anywhere other than where she was used to using drugs.

"You can show proof that you have just been released from prison, and on that one day you could ride for free anywhere," Donna explained.

Vanessa chimed in: "If you can't figure out what to do, if you're really hungry, find a hospital and tell the ER staff that you want to hurt yourself. You can have a bed and food for a couple of nights that way."

Hailey nodded as if she was taking mental notes of everything the women were saying. She seemed more confident after the women lovingly gave her advice.

But I stood back bewildered by the idea that Hailey might have to go to an ER to get food and fearful that this "plan" was no plan at all.

It was unthinkable for me.

Upon leaving prison, if they cannot get a bed at a halfway house many of the women will be offered some type of community resource by their probation officers. However, they will have trouble even accessing resources without money for transportation. They will also struggle to use resources like job fairs or counseling because they will be overwhelmed by the stress of finding food (keeping track of food pantry schedules and getting to them is a job in itself) and trying to reconnect with their children—and they will be low on sleep. Most places where the women will sleep upon leaving prison will involve multiple beds in one room or couch-surfing. Most will find it incredibly difficult to ever surpass these challenges because most companies that pay a living wage do not hire people who have been in prison.

One Wednesday night, Sydney shared a poem she had written. Her poem began with her recalling being locked in her bedroom at age five and having to pee in a corner of the bedroom because she had been left alone so long.

The poem shared other experiences, but after she described this, all I could see in my mind's eye was her as a little girl, squatting in a bedroom corner, terrified, confused, alone.

The women I met in prison seemed to have several main things in common that were likely sources of their suicidal thoughts and substance use.

They had a history of complex traumas, dysfunctional and abusive relationships, low self-worth, and massive amounts of shame.

Dealing with past trauma is a major component of recovery from addiction, but most of these women had never been given any real opportunity to heal from past trauma. And everything else followed.

For the women affected by suicidal thoughts, such thinking

seemed to be a desperate cry for relief and eventual escape from the chaos and hardship that consumed their lives, hardship that began when they were young children and continued into the present, in prison.

On another night, Jade came to Bible study for the first time and recognized another woman in the room even though they had not seen each other in years. When I asked how they knew each other, they explained that they had spent time in the same group home when they were kids.

Since I had known most of the women in the room for several months, I asked if any of the other women had ever spent time in a children's group home or foster care.

Nearly every hand went up.

After hearing these women's stories, it became clearer to me what these women really needed. These women needed meaningful relationships that did not involve substance use. They needed basic needs met—food, housing, work—so they did not have to live paralyzed by stress and overwhelmed with worry. The women needed opportunities to exercise their own agency, to be able to make decisions about what happened to them and some control over where their lives were headed. And they were desperate for relief from the terror and shame of the physical and sexual traumas they had endured, so they needed a pathway to genuine healing.

Ultimately, I realized the prison system is fundamentally flawed. It is not simply a matter of prison reform. People who are addicted to substances and who are suicidal need things that a prison cannot give.

Prison sobers people up and puts them out of sight, but prison provides very little in the way of relationship. Therapists and chaplains are overextended, and phone calls are incredibly expensive.

At best, prison provides basic needs for the duration of people's sentences.

However, as just one example, the women had only light sweatshirts to wear outside during New England winters, and they had to go outside daily to get to the cafeteria.

In prison, there is little to no agency and a lack of genuine healing.

Time in prison may seem to outsiders like it is fixing a problem, but prison does not provide any sort of real response to the sources of these women's pain. And if pain isn't adequately addressed, cycles of trauma, poverty, mental distress, addiction, wounding actions, and prison time persist.

Looking around the circle, I asked the women, "What do you want God to do for you?"

We were in the middle of a Bible study series answering questions that Jesus actually asked in the Gospel accounts of his life. In three different gospels Jesus asks, "What do you want me to do for you?"

We all wrote responses to the question on Post-it Notes and then placed them on the walls around us. We had our backs to the notes we wrote. I talked about how we often struggle to name our deepest needs. Sometimes we even put our truest needs out of sight, trying to ignore them and imagining that no one, not even God, can help us with them.

I invited the women to share out loud what they had written on the notes if they wanted. And many did. Afterward, I encouraged them to take the notes off the wall and pile them on the floor in the middle of the room.

The floor was gross, like it was most Wednesday evenings. It is only vacuumed every few months.

There were hundreds of dead bugs along the baseboards. Bits of paper and tons of dust and dirt were scattered across the carpet.

The notes were all piled together, and I asked my Bible study coleader, Jacob, to pray over the pile. I said that praying and offering these things to God was a step forward because we were acknowledging our needs and the power these needs have in our lives and because we were allowing the Spirit of God to offer us grace and love in the midst of our deepest needs.

"Can I get on my knees?"

If you listened to Ms. Aaliyah attentively, she would often inspire you, as she did me in this moment.

She knew Scripture well. She frequently made astute observations. Regularly, when women shared painful stories, she was the first to comfort them.

I responded, "Yes. Of course, you can get on your knees." And before thinking I also said, "I will get on my knees with you."

Then I hesitated.

I looked around at the disgusting mess on the floor. I thought about how long it had been since it had been cleaned and looked around for dead bugs right beneath me.

But Ms. Aaliyah did not even pause.

She immediately went to her knees and buried her head into the chair she had been sitting on. So I followed her lead and got on my knees too.

Jacob began praying earnestly for all of us, for the notes, for the things that we needed God to do for us. As Jacob prayed, I peeked.

I opened my eyes to find that nearly every woman in the room had also gotten on her knees.

Testimony time was an especially meaningful part of the evening. Women shared stories from the past week, and we all listened attentively to one another, open to what we might learn, open to how we might be changed by what we heard, aiming to practice the faithful presence that we all desperately needed for our healing.

I remember the night that Cheryl used her testimony time to express gratitude for her "bunkie," a term the women used to describe their cellmates. Their capacity to humanize one another in a situation that was so dehumanizing always amazed me.

"My bunkie reads a Bible story or a few verses from the Bible to me every night. She always explains what the story or verses mean so that I can understand. Then she prays for me too, right before I go to sleep. I want to thank God for her," Cheryl said.

Immediately, my heart filled with warm delight as I imagined these two women talking about God and the Bible and praying together in their prison cell.

"I did not know much about God before coming to prison, but because of my bunkie I know a lot more now. I even call my boyfriend each week to tell him Bible passages to read," she said.

Then she shared how her bunkie described the Trinity to her.

Cheryl recalled, "She talked about that, you know, the three things? She explained that there is God and what are the other two? [other women in the room responded to her]. Oh yes, the Son and the Spirit. My bunkie said God is like the light switch in our cell—the source of the light—and the Spirit is like the voltage going across our ceiling and Jesus is the light."

If people who are incarcerated get anything out of prison, it is because those same people somehow find a way—in the midst of demoralizing, debasing conditions—to embody hope for one another.

At first, singing was my least favorite part of leading Bible study because I was incredibly self-conscious. Over time, it became my favorite part of the evening. The women would sing loudly and unashamedly, even if not on pitch, and I began to mirror them.

I guess one Wednesday night along the way, I realized that they were not insecure. Why did I need to be? We do not usually recognize that we enjoy having permission to be ourselves until we get that permission. When we do, it is incredibly freeing.

It is ironic for me to describe "finding freedom" behind so many locked doors. It is likely because I walked out at the end of every Wednesday evening.

Another reason I grew to love singing was because I stopped leading it most of the time. As it turned out, other women in the room had incredible gifts for leading music, and some had remarkable voices. I could just sit back and enjoy being led.

And I also learned to love it because of the transformation that happened in the room when we sang. We all came alive. It is as if the music was revival water for the dead parts of our souls.

We frequently sang a song called "Spring Up, Oh Well."

I sang this song many times, first as a child at camp, then at youth group, and then as a camp counselor while a college student. But of course, the line where we sing, "I've got a river of life flowing out of me . . . opens prison doors, sets the captives free," has a different tonality, a far different meaning, when you sing it with exuberance together with women who are *literally* in prison.

One evening, we sang "This Little Light of Mine" especially passionately. We had begun the tradition, started by one of the women, of having different people in the circle create their own line to the song and then we would join in. For example, a woman might call out, "All up in this place," and we would chime in, "I'm gonna let it shine!"

This particular night, everyone was out of their seats, and we were jumping and dancing and singing "This Little Light of Mine" so loudly that one of the corrections officers came into the room. She watched what was happening with amazement. She joined us and started clapping her hands and smiling.

Joy gathers.

As we sang, our ashes seemed to become crowns of beauty, our mourning turned to joy, and our spirits of despair transformed into praise.

Our music became an act of resistance to all of the forms of death that had happened and were happening in our lives. Our singing turned into embodied opposition to our fear, anger, and profound loss. Our joyful noise opposed the imprisonment of bodies, minds, and hearts.

Suddenly, we were rejoicing in what ought to be.

Our dancing, jumping, clapping, and singing together pushed against voices that declared "You are alone," "You are worthless," or "There is no hope."

The louder we sang and declared new truths, the more the voices saying to us, "You do not matter," "Your grief will never lift," or "Your struggle will never be overcome" were quieted.

It was healing joy.

In the very act of gathering—of committing to rejoice and to recognize what is good and true, and to declare our meaning and dignity through God's love—we were participating in the very joy of God.

And it was there, assembled with these women, jumping and dancing in the air and clapping my hands boisterously, singing at the top of my lungs, that I realized they were my cloud of witnesses.

Suddenly, I felt like the prophet Elisha's servant.

One morning, Elisha and his servant were surrounded by a strong force of people, with horses and chariots, who were trying to find and kill them.

I had felt on many days as if I too was surrounded by a strong force and needed to remain prepared for imminent disaster and death.

I had been living this way for months.

Elisha asked God to open his servant's eyes so that they could see what Elisha saw. The servant's eyes were opened, and the servant saw that those who were with them were more than those who were against them; there were horses and chariots of fire all around Elisha.

As I looked at these women—this cloud of witnesses dancing around me—I saw something like what Elisha and the servant had seen.

It was as if God whispered, "You're not defenseless."

There was something beyond what I had been able to recognize previously.

And it is the *something more*—which surrounds current

circumstances, is the invisible connection between human beings, is deeper than what the eye can actually see—that makes
life meaningful.

While singing in this room, the something more of God—of
love that is worth praying for, worth seeking, worth living for—
was so real to me.

After Elisha and his servant saw the something more, Elisha
asked God to blind the army that was trying to kill them, and rather
than leading the army where they intended to go Elisha took them to
a different place. Elisha led the blinded army into its enemy's city.

When those in the army arrived and their eyes were opened,
they realized they were suddenly the vulnerable ones. I imagine
they were terrified.

But when the king of Israel asked Elisha whether everyone
in the army should be killed, Elisha responded with a wild idea.
Elisha said they should be fed and freed.

And so the king provided a feast.

And the men went away.

It is a mysterious, miraculous turn of events. Nourishment
and life instead of retribution and death. Right there in the middle of the Old Testament.

That's the gift of being able to see the something more,
I suppose.

For the next couple of months at Bible study, we discussed the
fruit of the Spirit: love, joy, peace, patience, kindness, goodness,
faithfulness, gentleness, and self-control.

One evening, we were discussing goodness, and I asked the
group, "Who has been good to you?"

Theresa quickly replied that the Bible study leaders had been
good to her. She said, "You use our first names. You listen to us.
You care about and see us."

Tears of *joy* welled up in my eyes. So simple yet so profound.
She went on: "Every time you come here a little bit of my hu-

manity is restored. Every Wednesday night I get a little bit of my dignity back."

We looked at her and tried to express how thankful we were for her words. What she did not know and I should have said is that I felt the same way about her and the other women who came to the group. They had been so good to me.

Week after week, these women witnessed to God's faithfulness, trusted God, cried out to God, and believed the promises of Scripture. I clung to their hope and convictions until mine came back. I did not have much faith during those first months of visiting the prison, but these women held faith for me.

Like the friends who took the man on the mat to Jesus, their faith was healing me.

As I spent more and more time with them, I realized the helpful help I had needed most was a group of people who sat in faithful presence with one another.

Every time I shared space with the women I got less angry, I became more courageous, I got a little more in touch with my humanity. My soul became increasingly open to joy.

My very first night at the prison I met Gloria.

She walked in and sat right next to me. The chairs were all touching in the circle. One of her arms—covered in scars, white lines all up and down her forearm from cuts of self-harm—rested gently against my own.

Immediately, her pain was evident.

Gloria had just had a baby three months before, while in a prison. She had told several prison staff members for a couple of days that she would go into labor soon and needed help, but no one believed her. The morning that she had her baby she was forced to follow the usual prison routine, including walking to the cafeteria, while in labor.

Gloria put a shirt between her legs to catch the fluids leaking from her body. She made it to the cafeteria and back by leaning against walls.

She called on the corrections officers for help several times during the previous night and that morning, but they kept telling her that the doctor would not be in until later.

Mid-morning, Gloria had her baby on her own, in her cell, with her roommate watching.

Gloria was one of the first people to share during Bible study that night. She cried profusely. She talked about the darkness she felt, how alone she felt. She told us she stared at pictures sent to her of her baby. She told us how she longed to hold her baby. Gloria was traumatized and heartbroken.

She missed her baby terribly; she had endured so much, too much. Her profound grief and trauma made her want to die by suicide.

I had decided on the way to the prison that first night that I would just watch and learn how the team leads the Bible study. But I unexpectedly found myself asking Gloria if I could pray for her. It was a visceral response to her pain, and I did not know what else to do.

I prayed the most earnest, honest prayer that I had prayed since Dad died.

"What is the difference between a cry of pain that is also a cry of praise and the cry of pain that is pure despair? Faith? The cry of faith, even if it is a cry against God, moves toward God, has its meaning in God, as in the cries of Job," writes the poet Christian Wiman.

After the prayer Gloria left, overwhelmed.

Gloria regularly attended Bible study. A few months later, when she walked in, I said, "Hey Gloria, welcome. I am glad you are here." It was my routine greeting.

"I am glad to be here too! It is my birthday today," she remarked.

"Awesome! How old are you?" I asked excitedly.

"I am twenty-one!"

I told her that this was a great night and we were going to celebrate her. After the other women signed in and took their seats, I invited everyone to sing "Happy Birthday" to her, and then I asked Gloria if she had a song request since she loves music. I said that this could be our birthday gift to her.

She chose the song "I Know I've Been Changed."

Thankfully, Naomi, who is incredibly gifted at leading people in music, was also present. She has a beautiful voice and an infectious charisma, and she got most of us on our feet. Naomi encouraged everyone to sing loudly, moving her arms like a choir director.

Naomi can play the drums too, so she walked toward one side of the room and put her hands on the window sill. As she moved them up and down, she created a loud, powerful beat for us to follow as we sang. The drumming of her hands filled the room, and those of us who were standing began to dance.

We really got into the song, especially the birthday girl. Gloria was dancing and jumping and spinning with her hands in the air. Nearly every person in the room was clapping to Naomi's drum beat and belting out the song. We were loud and we were rejoicing. It was a beautiful sight.

Right as the song finished, Gloria, overcome by emotion, sat down in her plastic chair and wept uncontrollably.

We quickly all sat down, too, and got really quiet.

Eventually, women began acknowledging Gloria's tears and saying things like, "I know it is so hard to be away from family on your birthday," and, "We love you." "We have your back. It's going to be okay."

We thought she was sad to be away from people she loved on her birthday.

She continued to weep.

Since she was crying so forcefully, I could not go on with the other elements of the Bible study, and so I did the only thing

I knew to do. I did what I had done that first night I met her. I motioned to everyone that I was going to pray. I thanked God for her life and for her baby. I thanked God she was born, and I asked God to take away her sorrow.

She continued to cry.

After I said "amen," I looked up and noticed she was slowly waving her arm back and forth over her head, giving the impression that I had missed something. I realized she wanted to talk.

We all grew quiet again. You could have heard a pin drop.

She tried to take in a few deeper breaths. When she could speak, she softly said, "No, no, I'm not sad." She sobbed silently through the words. "I am crying because I have never felt God's presence before. I have never felt God like that."

She took a few more deep breaths and went on. "No, no, I'm not sad." She took in more air.

"*I'm overwhelmed with joy.*"

Through Gloria's words, her conviction, suddenly I too was arrested by joy.

Joy has a wondrous way of seizing our attention. It often comes swiftly and powerfully. Joy can be a gift of the breaking in of goodness, beauty, and truth amid brokenness.

In Greek, the language of most of the New Testament, "the word for joy (*chara*) is connected to and sometimes not clearly distinguished from 'grace' (*charis*), the gift that is freely given."

Gloria did not know that I was on a team researching joy.

The fact that she used the word "joy," a word that is not used all that often to describe how we feel, astounded me.

I looked around the room, noticing that the other women and my teammates were also in awe after what had just happened. One by one we all smiled widely, some of us crying tears of joy like Gloria. We could not help but feel joy, too, to rejoice at the birthday gift that God had given her.

Joy is infectious.

Joy has a "too-muchness" about it. Life often leaves us with the feeling of scarcity, but when we look for, recognize, embrace, and give ourselves over to joy—when we feel it deep in our bones, deep in our hearts, it is often so big that it feels like we cannot help but allow joy to seep out of our bodies and be shared with others.

Joy is an experience of connectedness to others, to God, and to meaning that both roots us and transcends us, so it is both orienting and disorienting.

There were no balloons. We did not have a cake or candles. But we had one another.

We were not alone. We were not defenseless. And for this moment we were not sad either.

We too became overwhelmed with joy.

It was in this prison, listening to and looking on at these women's strength and resilience, that I was inspired to respond to theologian Willie Jennings's concept of making pain productive without justifying or glorifying suffering. Against all logic, inside of a barbed wire fence, I began to grasp the work of joy.

And in a grimy room with stained floors and plastic chairs, the sheer silence of the previous year and a half became fire.

6

The Search

About midnight Paul and Silas were praying and singing hymns to God, and the prisoners were listening to them. Suddenly there was an earthquake, so violent that the foundations of the prison were shaken; and immediately all the doors were opened and everyone's chains were unfastened. When the jailer woke up and saw the prison doors wide open, he drew his sword and was about to kill himself, since he supposed that the prisoners had escaped. But Paul shouted in a loud voice, "Do not harm yourself, for we are all here."

—Acts 16:25–28

"**I** tried to hang up last week."

Hang up was the phrase women used in the prison to describe the act of trying to hang themselves in their cell. Jayla went on to casually explain, "I coded, and they brought me back to life. So that's why I can be here with you all this week." She said it matter-of-factly, without intonation, as if she was simply telling us what she ate for breakfast.

As lovingly as possible, I asked her what was going through her mind when she decided to kill herself.

"I have been prostituting since I was seventeen. I am thirty years old. I am homeless. What is there to live for?"

The circle of women around her sat in silence for what felt like too long.

For every suicide in the United States, twenty-five more people attempt suicide. Suicidal thinking is highest among people *between the ages of eighteen and twenty-five years old*, but each year millions of Americans of all different age groups, like Jayla, have serious thoughts about taking their own life. While young people report thinking about suicide more than any other age group, in 2017 suicide rates were highest among females between forty-five and fifty-four and men over sixty-five.

After some moments of silence, we looked at Jayla and tried to express how grateful we were that her life had been saved. We told her we loved her and would have missed her terribly. Several of the women compassionately shared stories about what Jayla had done for them in recent weeks. We explained why she mattered to us.

The joy of the evening of Gloria's birthday felt distant on this night.

Jayla wanted relief from a life that constantly broke her heart. She was not the only one in the Bible study group who felt this way.

One Wednesday evening, Amy explained that she had come to Bible study only because her "rec time" had been taken away.

Rec time, short for recreational time, was precious time in the prison. It was the two hours a day that the women could shower, call approved family or friends (on those people's dimes), and gather around tables to talk.

"My rec time was taken away because I broke a prison rule, but the COs (corrections officers) said I could still come to Bible study. I had only been to church twice in my life, and both times were in prison just two weeks before my first night here," Amy recalled, chuckling.

Then she softened her voice: "I had never read the Bible and didn't know a thing about Christianity, but I came so I could get out of my room." She said it like she was in a confessional booth with a priest, like she had been keeping a secret, as if it were wrong to come to Bible study without a desire to be there or a background in faith.

Then her tone totally changed, like she was revealing a beautiful surprise: "But I love this! I can't get enough of it. I want to keep coming back."

And she did. Amy kept coming week after week. Just as she had the first night, she sat on the edge of her seat every Wednesday. Her genuine spiritual wonder and excitement were demonstrable and intense.

One night I looked at her and tried to remember the last time I had sat on the edge of my seat like that—so genuinely open.

I could not remember.

Over time Amy became totally captivated by stories in the Bible and, I think, by the larger narrative of meaning for life that they offer. She was always absorbed in whatever conversation we were having, and she constantly responded kindly to the other women in the room. She learned the songs we sang and contributed her ideas and stories and questions.

Sometimes, Amy's reflections were full of pain—the anguish that accompanies growing up with a mother overcome by addiction to drugs.

Her stories revealed the hurt of not having had the chance to finish high school or truly celebrate being young and innocent. Often, the effects of her own substance use and subsequent joblessness and homelessness would reveal themselves in her words, mostly in the form of self-loathing.

Like Jayla, Amy had no real sense of home—physical, emotional, or existential—and she had also done sex work to get what she needed to survive. And like Jayla, Amy hated herself for it.

Week after week Amy talked about the desire to forgive herself—for numerous things. She believed her addictions and her suicidal thoughts were moral failures because they were connected to her inability to be a good person. We kept trying to explain to her that these were instead health issues, but society had taught her otherwise.

Between having had sex for money, being addicted to substances, having considered suicide, and ending up in prison, Amy felt intense shame. She saw herself as a living disappointment—to herself, to others, and to God.

We tried to help Amy see that her addiction (and consequent sex work) and suicidal thoughts were directly related to her upbringing and the many traumas she had endured that needed healing. We wanted to help her see that her addiction and suicidal thoughts were related to pain and that it was her pain that had to be addressed for her recovery to be long term.

We would tell her again and again that God loved her and we loved her.

She wanted to believe us, and she would for a night, sometimes for a few weeks, but the group could invest in her only one or two hours each week. The other hours in prison always seemed to undo any growth in loving herself that was produced.

The shame always crept back in, and she would be disgusted with herself. She constantly asked us to pray that she would learn to love herself. And I did. I prayed earnestly every week, at home and at the prison. The whole team prayed constantly for her.

One night, she did not show up to Bible Study, and her roommate, Jordan, asked to share something about Amy. Jordan began intensely crying. She explained that Amy tried to kill herself and that, thankfully, she had been rescued, but she was in mental health.

Mental health is a special unit in the prison where women who actively threatened to or attempted to die by suicide are separated from the general population, put into straitjackets, and closely monitored. Once they are deemed healthy enough to return to the general population, they remain on suicide watch, but as a group, still with restrictions but not as severe.

Through Jordan's sobs she described how Amy had been bullied in prison recently and that it had become too much.

As she had been culturally trained, Jordan was ashamed of her tears. She said no one really makes her cry but that this was Amy, and Amy was really special, and no one should have treated her that way. Jordan said she would not have known what to do with herself if Amy had died.

I would not have known what to do with myself either.

And like Jordan, I was brokenhearted over the way Amy felt about herself. I cried as Jordan cried. We all knew how much Amy was trying to learn to love herself, and we were horrified to discover that other human beings were treating Amy so poorly and deepening her self-hatred. It was the last thing she needed in the midst of the shame she lived with.

I wept for Amy's pain, and I wept that we had come so close to losing her. My heart ached thinking about where she was that night. I knew she needed care that was far different than a straitjacket.

Hearing women speak so candidly about their suicidal thoughts was by far the hardest thing about leading Bible study at the prison.

Often, as I made my way there on Wednesday nights I'd clutch my hands on the steering wheel or, if another person was driving, tightly grip the loose-leaf papers. I imagined that I was clinging to life for my friends, afraid of who might not show up, even more afraid of why.

The women's addiction issues and suicidal thoughts called to me in the fog of grief. I became desperate to learn what people can do to meaningfully respond.

And I wondered what our exploration of joy might offer in light of these major issues. Might the quest for joy be part of a real, valuable response?

I knew that opioids and suicide were killing people at alarming rates, and I suddenly wondered how these forms of death might be related—not just in my own life, not just in Jayla's and Amy's lives, but in the fuller picture of what was happening in America.

I began doggedly reading about and reflecting on the surge in opioid overdoses and suicides. As it turns out, heroin users are much more likely than others to die by suicide.

Of course, there is more to the story.

I scanned pictures on a webpage of people who had died from opioid overdose. I was struck, not just by Laura Hope's age, but also by her photo. Her thick brown eyebrows, braces, and powder-puff football getup revealed her youthfulness and reminded me of girls I knew in high school. Laura Hope was raised in Atlanta, Georgia.

Heartbreakingly, Laura Hope Laws died at seventeen of a toxic mix of substances during her senior year of high school.

Her dad, David Laws, was willing to reflect on her via Zoom with me and my research assistant, fittingly named Joy.

I logged in and took a deep breath as Joy and I prepared to ask him questions. He was sitting at his home office desk. He was wearing a button-up shirt and silver-rimmed oval glasses, and he had a full beard of mixed brown and gray hair. On a mantle behind him were all sorts of framed pictures of his three children, showing just above his head.

"Could you tell us who Laura Hope was? What was she like?" Joy asked.

David's face lit up as he described a teenager who was indiscriminate with her friendships and who was a varsity athlete as a freshman.

"Laura Hope enjoyed playing sports, was an active member of her youth group in Georgia, and loved to help other people," he explained.

Chapter 6

David's joy was palpable, even through the laptop screen.

A few minutes later, David showed us a photo of Laura Hope as an eight-year-old. He commented on the expression on her face, saying, "She was like, 'I'm here. What's up?'" He chuckled to himself softly, and his face suggested that he was recalling what it felt like to rejoice over her when she was a young child.

David told us that when he stumbled across the photo, it made him laugh and smile because "she was so darn cute in the photo." He keeps it in his office so he can regularly look at it.

Laura Hope was fourteen when she was given prescription opioids to manage her pain after her jaw was broken while playing soccer. Being given prescription opioids before twenty-two years old dramatically increases risk for addiction, especially if the young person is already facing other stressors like trauma and trouble with school, both of which Laura Hope dealt with.

Her story isn't uncommon. Misuse of prescription opioids is the strongest predictor of heroin use, and youths who are especially susceptible to addiction are those who lack social support or healthy coping skills.

Addiction is widespread in her family, so David said that substances were a natural go-to, especially during difficult times. David told us that Laura Hope had been sent to an alternative school for an incident related to weed, and that made her feel shunned.

"What Laura Hope needed was extra support, without being ostracized," he reflected.

By age sixteen, David said, Laura Hope had suffered tremendously. One of her closest friends died by suicide, another friend died from overdose, and another friend whom she was in love with died of brain cancer.

Substances (especially heroin) were a way that Laura Hope could feel normal and try to make the pain go away—pain that David thinks was associated with the suffering she had endured, her struggles in school, and her growing insecurity about her own identity.

It seems that for many people addiction to opioids begins like it did for Laura Hope and my dad—with pain that they desperately want to numb or escape.

Opiates produce feelings of euphoria, comfort, and pleasure, causing people to feel drowsy and relaxed. They bind to the areas of the brain that control pain and emotions, increasing dopamine, a hormone that makes us feel good. Since opioids feel so good—they give people the sense that they are warm and happy—they are a welcome relief when life is miserable.

For a time, opioids magically take away all pain—not just physical pain, but also emotional, psychological, and existential pain. And in place of pain people get the respite they have been searching for.

Taking a long, hard look at America's opioid crisis exposes more than addiction. It reveals pain related to the very fabric of *our way of life*.

After watching a movie with one of her best friends, taking a college test, carefully buying thoughtful gifts for her beloved family members, and talking with her dad on the phone, Madison Holleran died by suicide near her college in Philadelphia. She was only nineteen years old, and it was her first year of college.

Several people have written about Madison's life and death. Her family has been courageously willing to talk about her suicide as part of their effort to reduce the number of suicides among college students.

Carli Bushoven, Madison's older sister, exchanged emails with Joy and me. Carli explained how sports affected Madison's confidence: "She started playing soccer in kindergarten, but by the time she was in high school she was the star—winning awards, getting county, and even state recognition. I think soccer and sports in general gave her confidence she was lacking as a child. She was suddenly outgoing, funny, popular, and silly."

Chapter 6

Madison became a star soccer player and a successful middle-distance runner in high school. She was offered scholarships in both sports, but she chose to pursue her second favorite sport because she could not resist attending the University of Pennsylvania, an Ivy League school.

Madison left a book, *Reconstructing Amelia*, near where she died. It tells the story of a girl who jumps off a building. At the end of the book Amelia's mother learns that she did not jump; rather, she had been pushed.

It is impossible to know exactly why Madison left this book, but it seems she was trying to send a message that dying by suicide was something she felt forced to do—by what, exactly, or why is impossible to know.

When Joy and I asked Carli to tell us about Madison, Carli reflected on what she was like as a child. Madison was the middle child, number three of five siblings. Carli says her room was always the messiest in the house. "It was almost like all her effort and energy went into sports and academics, so there wasn't any time left over for organization," Carli explained.

Carli's favorite memories of Madison are of all of the siblings together during the holidays:

> All the siblings loved sleeping on the pull-out couch in the family room on Christmas eve. We could fall asleep watching a Christmas movie, with the fire still going, always hoping to catch our parents putting gifts under the tree in the middle of the night or stuff our stockings. In the morning, we would open presents and mom would make pancakes. I think a lot of people have fond memories of Christmas when they were little, but it really stands out to me because we were all together, we were happy and life just seemed easy.

While she grew up in a big, loving family and enjoyed athletic successes in high school, after Madison went to college she began saying things like, "Something isn't right. I don't feel right. I don't feel like myself."

Carli went on to explain: "The changes in our loved ones can be subtle, but they are still signs and symptoms and we need to be aware of that. Having an open and honest conversation and not being afraid to bring up depression, bipolar, anxiety, suicidal thoughts, is important."

We asked Carli, "If you could cause everyone in America to take one step in the right direction towards lessening suicide, what would you have us do?"

She responded directly: "Have more open and honest conversations with the people you love. . . . Open up, have a conversation and ask the hard questions."

In one of the last photos that Madison shared on Instagram, she is posing with a friend at a party—Madison has her arms around her neck—with a huge smile. Everyone around her seems to be having a good time too. The rest of her Instagram photos demonstrate a similar happiness—poses at cross country meets and other events, friends huddled together, friends playing dress-up for Halloween and enjoying being young.

That is what it looks like anyway.

Madison's happy posts reminded me of a book I had read.

Researcher Donna Freitas talked with college students at thirteen campuses (big and small, Ivy league and community colleges, faith-based and secular) about social media. The overall consensus was that college students feel like they are constantly being watched and that the people observing them—family members, peers, future employers—expect them to always appear happy, effective, and passionate about everything they do.

For most of the college students Freitas talked with, this translates to constantly posting online about how much they are enjoying life and how fabulously successful they are. Freitas also found the college students she talked with are desperate to avoid letting peers see any signs of weakness or failure.

Freitas realized that feelings of inadequacy rise up when constantly posting about happiness. College students compare how happy they actually feel with all of their friends' endless happy posts and even their own happy posts, and they feel inferior to both—because they do not think they are as happy as their friends are and they also do not feel as happy as they are telling everyone that they are.

Freitas calls it *the happiness effect*.

Keeping up an appearance of happiness can cause young people to feel like they are being fake in a culture that highly values authenticity. For many young people today, life is depressing, even pointless, if you cannot be true to yourself. Since authenticity *is* the good life, life cannot be good if you cannot be authentically yourself.

Young people are also struggling to even define happiness (or unhappiness), which is also part of the problem. It is difficult to find happiness if you do not know what you are looking for.

On Ivy League campuses and in middle- and upper-class communities, people have developed extraordinary expectations for what a happy, good life is.

While I was teaching Life Worth Living at Yale, this became increasingly clear.

Happiness is being associated with success, which basically means high-impact achievements, visibility, and wealth. Each one of these markers of success is an extremely difficult target.

High impact is an arbitrary goal, but more and more people describe *the* life worth living as having impact. There is a sense that people who live the best lives are those who leave a mark that is worth talking about and idealizing.

Increasingly, young people are realizing no one will talk about what they are doing if they don't advertise it. So young people feel pressure to have a good personal branding strategy.

I wrote about the weight of seeing yourself as a brand in *Always On*:

> Like a good brand, you should describe yourself and write storylines that support how you want your audience to perceive you. Why are you important? What sort of value do you add? Why are you unique? Other online activities, like tagging, signifying location, filtering, and editing, also help you curate your

brand. You can tag certain people that you want your brand to be affiliated with, people who will raise the value of your brand. You can check into locations and events that support the ways you describe yourself and the stories you tell. You can filter your photos and edit your videos to present yourself to your audience.

It is awful to imagine youth obsessing over these options, struggling with these overwhelming questions and trying to market their lives as if they were products instead of human beings. Trying to increase visibility or give the right impression by carefully managing one's personal brand is stressful and anxiety-producing.

Desiring high-impact achievements, visibility, and wealth to feel happy is a toxic combination that can contribute to mental distress.

Not only do we live in an age of endless striving for personal happiness, but many communities, like college campuses, have also individualized the task of pursuing happiness. You are made to believe that you are in charge of your own happiness. Popular sentiments are "If I am not living the kind of life I ought to live, it is my fault" and "If I am not happy, it is because I have not tried hard enough."

We pursue a happy life, alone. And we call this liberty.

Beyond what I have just described, too many people also don't recognize that there may be something worth desiring that is worthier than happiness, high-impact achievements, visibility, or wealth.

And even if we have an inkling that there is something worthier to pursue, too many of us are not sure what it is.

Lynn, forty years old, walked into my office wearing a dark-colored suit and a bright, colorful tie. He looked sharp and he spoke in a captivating way—evidence of a man who reads a lot and is paid to talk in front of people every week behind a pulpit.

Joy knew that Lynn had been through unimaginable grief in the previous two years and asked if he would be willing to talk with us. For over two hours we asked Lynn questions about his loved ones, and his reflections on their lives and deaths further kindled the fiery passion inside me to be part of a groundswell of people devoted to reducing suicide and addiction.

When Lynn started talking about his little brother, Chris, whom everyone lovingly called "Pookah," a grin came over his face, as if a thousand beautiful memories had flooded his mind all at once.

Pookah was six feet six, so everyone expected him to play basketball, and he did, but Lynn said Pookah's real passion was cooking. He went to culinary school and loved to create Cajun dishes and southern soul food. Growing up, Pookah enjoyed miming in church to express his pain and joy. "He was a mixed variety of an individual," Lynn explained.

It became clear as we talked that Lynn has always been the caretaker of his siblings. Pookah saw Lynn as a father figure.

Throughout the conversation Lynn discussed how crack, alcohol, and marijuana had affected many members of his family and consequently their relationships. "We cannot escape our life," Lynn explained before compellingly quoting the rapper Lecrae: "Rich man need a vacation, hop a plane. Broke man need a vacation, Mary Jane." He followed the quote by saying, "That was my brother. He could not find a way to untangle everything or feel confident. He was tied to substances."

Lynn believed Pookah felt he had to lift himself up with substances and that "it did not matter that it was a false joy."

Lynn believed Pookah became angry after growing up seeing the hypocrisy of family members as well as the inability of people in his community to be truly liberated. "Pookah wanted to know why God had not produced a liberation that people could touch and feel. As Pookah got older, he discovered holes in society, faith, and family life that he could not ignore—holes that made him feel hopeless," Lynn said.

Lynn and Pookah talked a lot about these holes, his questions, and his frustrations.

In November of 2017, Pookah's world came crashing down. He lost his job, which from Lynn's perspective Pookah tied to his ability to provide and "be a real man"; wrecked his car, which Lynn said helped him to have a sense of confidence; and lost his girlfriend—the first girl he had ever told Lynn he loved, who broke up with him.

"All of these were symbols of his identity. Pookah tried to express to people that he was troubled, but overall, it was not received well," Lynn recalled.

Lynn explained that in his family, "There is no space for weakness, especially in men. No whining, no flinching." And when Pookah sent a video to his ex-girlfriend telling her that he was going to kill himself, she texted a question.

"Where can I bring your stuff?"

Shortly after, she left his things in a box on his porch. Perhaps she did not imagine that he was serious.

That evening, Pookah gathered with his family to watch the Dallas Cowboys play the Philadelphia Eagles. Lynn said he was perfectly normal during the game. "He rooted for anyone playing the Cowboys and he talked noise that evening like he always did. Nothing that night seemed like anything bad was going to happen," Lynn recalled.

The next morning Lynn's father called him asking if Lynn had seen Pookah, and Lynn had not. His dad called back just thirty minutes later to tell Lynn that he found Pookah dead at his house. Lynn said he did not even wait for his dad to finish the call. He hung up the phone and drove to his house in a haze.

The police would not let him see Pookah until he was on a gurney. Lynn was devastated. He officiated his funeral a few days later.

Lynn spent the year after Pookah's death pastoring the family and trying to foster healing in everyone else before he realized his need for counseling and started going to therapy, "trying to find balance between mind, body, soul."

Then, a few months into therapy, Lynn's wife came home from

the store and told him he should reach out to Charles, his best friend of seventeen years.

Charles and Lynn celebrated holidays together, preached annually at each other's churches, and frequently had coffee conversations. Lynn said that after seventeen years of close friendship Charles was another brother to him.

Charles was a husband and father of four children, a pastor and a community activist who also ran a food bank. From Lynn's perspective he was doing all kinds of things to give to others, but "he was giving of himself from a space he did not have, even to the detriment of himself."

When Lynn's wife talked to Charles in the store, he was buying his daughter a cake and ice cream for her birthday. Charles said that was all he could afford, and Lynn's wife could tell that he was down. So she came home and told Lynn he needed to reach out to Charles.

Charles openly said things "were not okay but that God would provide."

Since Lynn had been dealing with Pookah's death while working and in seminary, he had not connected as much with Charles as they had in all those years before, but Lynn told his wife that he would reach out to Charles during the seminary's spring break.

Spring break was just a few weeks away.

But a few days later, Lynn received a call that Charles had died by suicide.

Shocked and heartbroken after his death, Lynn desired understanding, so he talked with people in order to try to make sense of what had happened.

Charles had been making a salary in the $70,000s as an associate pastor but then decided to become the lead pastor at a new little church. By the time he died, he was making a salary in the $20,000 range, and his wife had been ill, so she could not work. Apparently, Charles's house was about to be taken away, but he did not feel like he could ask anyone else for help.

Lynn said Charles had likely gotten to the point where he had believed "God would come through and everything would be okay—a type of dysfunctional prosperity gospel—as if he had the ability to command God like a genie." Lynn knows this sort of thinking about God was deeply rooted for Charles and feels that his friend's misguided understanding of God failed him.

"Charles came to the end of a God who could," Lynn explained.

Lynn believes that Charles thought that God was present, but that God could not see him; he had accepted that things were not going to change.

Like Pookah, right before his suicide Charles had been struggling financially and feeling like he was losing the self he had worked to create. Like Pookah, Charles also reached out to others. After his death, Lynn found out Charles had even told a mutual friend that he was thinking about killing himself.

There were several moments while listening to Lynn when my heart grew heavy. There were several times during the conversation when his words deeply resonated with me.

Especially when he said that just two months after burying Charles he had to bury his cousin who was twenty-eight years old.

Three funerals of three people he loved.

Lynn told me that his cousin, Jazmine, adored being around family, especially her daughter. "She really enjoyed barbecues for the holidays." Though she loved her family, Jazmine was biracial and had identity issues throughout her life. She had been troubled since she was a teen, constantly wondering, "'Where do I fit in?' 'What are my norms?'" Lynn explained.

Pookah, Charles, and Jazmine all struggled with identity in different ways, but the search for identity was critical for each of them. From Lynn's perspective, it was a major factor in their suicides.

When talking about both Pookah and Jazmine, Lynn described the stress of "code-switching." He discussed how Black people in America struggle with fragmentation, constantly feeling like their humanity is not being affirmed.

Lynn explained that once Black young people do figure out, "Oh, this is who I am," they then often have to wonder, "Where is this version of me going to be accepted?" Or if they develop a sense of who they are and they then confidently try to be that person, they may find themselves rejected and left wondering, "Do I have to re-create myself?"

Lynn explained that Jazmine was in this space of frustration for a while.

Before dying by suicide, she had already made two other attempts. As was the case for Pookah and Charles, Lynn believes her suicidal thoughts did not receive adequate responses. Lynn felt that rather than trying to get to Jazmine's pain and to show her compassion, others responded punitively.

According to Lynn, the general response to Jazmine's suicide attempts was, "There is no space for you to be that vulnerable and that broken."

People instead wondered why Jazmine was struggling so openly.

After thinking about Jayla's and Amy's experiences and the conversations I had with David, Carli, and Lynn, it became more and more important for me to help people understand that overdose and suicide are not moral failures, but demonstrations of pain that have led to despair.

Deaths from both suicide and opioid overdose have even been referred to as "deaths of despair." Despair is an awful teacher, an indiscriminate parasite that feeds off of self-doubt, grief, anger, self-hatred, and fear—in short, it feeds off of people's pain.

As I reflected on the different experiences that had been shared with me inside the prison and beyond its walls, I realized several sources of pain had come up: abuse, neglect, trauma, perceived failure, lack of control, and financial stress as well as overwhelming feelings of anxiety, inadequacy, worthlessness, or shame.

These sources of pain often nurture loneliness. People believe (whether based on reality or imagination) that they are alone in their circumstances and feelings and that no one empathizes with them or can relate with them.

And the more I thought about it, it seemed that in the case of suicide a lot of these pains contributed to a crisis of identity, which is an especially critical and agonizing human experience that must be carefully attended to.

A crisis of identity can cause us to sense that our gifts, values, beliefs, or passions have mysteriously vanished. It can make us feel as if we can no longer find meaning in or create meaning from our activities and relationships.

For nearly a year and half after my weeks of hell, the research on joy and visions of the good life that I was a part of at Yale felt distant and irrelevant.

Suddenly, though, I realized why the Life Worth Living classroom was a unique space. There are few communities or occasions where people are literally invited to discuss and describe what a meaningful life is and what wholeness looks like, especially in light of suffering.

Unexpectedly, I also recognized joy is not just relevant for our culture obsessed with synthetic happiness and riddled with pain, isolation, and existential rootlessness; it is also something we desperately need to understand, be open to, and eventually identify and experience. And when joy finds us, we need to express it deeply and freely and give others permission to do the same.

When we do, we find out that joy, as the women in the prison Bible study showed me, is a counteragent to despair after all.

7

Bright Sorrow

I remember when we parted there was an awkward moment when the severity of my situation and our unfamiliarity with each other left us with no words, and in a gesture that I'm sure was completely unconscious, he placed his hand over his heart for just a second as a flicker of empathetic anguish crossed his face. It sliced right through me. It cut through the cloud I was living in and let the plain day pour its balm upon me. It was, I am sure, one of those moments when we enact and reflect a mercy and mystery that are greater than we are, when the void of God and the love of God, incomprehensible pain and the peace that passeth understanding, come together in a simple human act.

—Christian Wiman,
My Bright Abyss

There will be a day in each of our lives when the question "How does pain fit into a good life?" is especially urgent.

There will be a moment, as there was for me on the pavement in the church parking lot when I found out Dustin died, when the world will seemingly stop. It will feel as if your heart has broken, and you will need a vision of a life worth living that can endure suffering.

Maybe that day has come or passed and you sit there reading this book, feeling the urgency of this question.

It's important that we consider how pain relates to the circumstances, actions, and emotions in our vision of a meaningful life.

In light of suffering, what should we hope for?

Given that pain is a part of the reality of being human, how do we pursue wholeness?

If I feel anxious, depressed, ashamed, fearful, or angry, is it possible for life to still be good?

At some point we all have to wrestle with suffering and discern its place in the life worth living. We have to make some sort of sense of how pain relates to the larger story being told, and we have to discern where God is in the midst of suffering—lest we be consumed by it.

No vision of the true life is sustainable if it does not account for pain. By grappling with suffering we actually come to a clearer understanding of joy.

While we may be able to articulate and live toward a vision that can endure our moments on the pavement, in my own experience it is possible only when we make friends with mystery.

The Bible is not a Google map to the good life.

As I came to accept after my weeks of hell, the Bible is more like instructions for filing your taxes—you know it's saying something important (and it feels like it's talking about benefits and deductions), but it's unclear, frustrating, and it takes longer than you want it to.

And you've implicitly been trained to always wonder whether you did what you should have and whether you need an expert to help.

Rather than being some sort of checklist for becoming a holy person, the Bible is a bunch of stories about people who endured messy existences.

The more I read the Bible, the more I notice how often its stories end with questions rather than answers. Many stories have little or no resolution. You turn the page excited to find out what happened only to realize that Jesus has moved on to a different town.

Sometimes really beautiful things happen in the Bible. People who want to be healed are healed. And they literally jump for joy.

But the Bible is basically chock-full of people struggling to make it one more day, to do hard things, and to hear from God. People found themselves in massive storms, lions' dens, and brothels. They suffered infertility, moved from place to place unsure where they would find their next meal (there are quite a few refugees in the Bible), slept with other people's spouses, stole from their siblings, betrayed their closest friends, and gave away their baby boys so that they would not be murdered.

More often than not, the Bible tells the stories of people who, despite being led right to the edge of the promised land, never got to see it. They lost everything, from homes to temples to the meaning of life—and as I said, they wept, stridently.

I have continued to read the Bible (including its points of confusion and frustration) because I find it reassuring that there are other people who have lived who don't have everything figured out and who fail.

Ultimately, the Bible reminds me that there is a larger story being told. The voice of God speaks to me through its pages.

As I read it and look for this overarching narrative, I realize my story, my family's story, is part of an all-embracing story about how, somehow, God's unconditional love encompasses the world, things are being made new, dead things come back to life again, and life is worth living.

The Bible invites us to be discerning people—not just about the stories in its pages, but as we read, about the stories we live and encounter.

When we read Bible stories, it is important to be able to imagine being on the side of suffering *and* liberation, pain *and* healing, despair *and* joy.

As we reflect on Noah's ark, we must imagine both the joy of making it on the boat and the despair of being left off. As we see the walls of Jericho fall in our mind's eye, we should consider Joshua's team and those human beings buried under the rubble. As we imagine and study the woman at the well, we must also identify with her.

We need to be able to see our potential to be the good Samaritan, the person who walked by, the person lying in the ditch, and one of the robbers who put the person in the ditch.

As we engage in this kind of imaginative discernment as individuals and in community, biblical stories create a dialogue between the lives of the people we are reading about and our own lives.

We read the text and it reads us.

And it is here in the midst of faithfulness to this dialogue— genuinely open, carefully listening, steadfastly struggling with questions, trying this way and that way—that the Spirit of God quietly reveals this is how you love; what wholeness is; the shape of forgiveness; what it looks like to find meaning in the mess, to rejoice and resist despair, to embrace sorrow, to recognize the good, to stand in awe of beauty, to share in joy.

Along the way, the Spirit shapes and empowers us to become more human, more alive, more attuned to the something more.

Yes, the Bible is full of muddled, difficult stories throughout its various genres—poetry, wisdom, prophecy, narratives, letters—but through imaginative discernment I have also come to believe there are a few things in it that we can hold on to as we struggle to make sense of pain.

One thing is that God keeps showing up.

A few weeks before Easter—a little over a year after my weeks of hell and a couple of months before I went to the prison Bible study for the first time—a leader of the prayer ministry at our church asked for volunteers to pray on Easter Sunday. Every Sunday, members of our prayer team line the church wall, and people can go to them to be prayed for, for anything.

I assumed the person making the request thought there would be more people than usual on Easter asking for prayer, meaning they would need more people willing to line the wall that day.

I certainly did not want anyone praying for me; I was not even sure what I thought about prayer at this point. However, it seemed like a good thing to be willing to pray for others, especially on Easter. This seemed like something I should sign up for, but I did not want to do it alone.

I nudged Paul and told him we should sign up to pray when the clipboard got to us.

A week before Easter, we received an email that told us to show up at the church an hour before the service began. That's when we realized we had signed up to pray for *an hour* before the service rather than pray for five minutes over someone during the service.

I told Paul that this was not what I had signed up for and that I no longer wanted to do it. I told him I could not imagine what we would all pray about for an hour. I did not think I had anything to say to God, and I did not want to hear anyone else talk to God either, for fear they would say ridiculous things about God that I was not buying into at that point.

If someone prayed something like, "Thank you, God, that you don't give us more than we can handle," I knew I would need to leave and Easter would be ruined more than it already was. I just couldn't do it.

Of course, I was not talking to anyone at my church about any of these thoughts or feelings. There seemed to be no place to talk about such dark feelings.

Paul insisted that we go. He reminded me of the kind of people we say we are. We had said we would be there, and our yes should be yes.

On Easter Sunday, I wore a black outfit (*yes, really*) and begrudgingly made my way to the church. We found the group we were supposed to be praying with and huddled next to them. The music team was practicing while people began taking turns praying, and they were so loud that I could not hear anything anyone said. I thought, "Thank God I cannot hear anyone talking foolishly about faith."

Obviously, I was grieving.

It was Easter Sunday, and I was annoyed that I had been tricked into praying for an hour. The leader of the group motioned that we should all get up. I was excited. I thought it was fantastic that our prayer time had been cut short. I was relieved and happy that I had survived the ten minutes of prayer, never hearing anyone or having to actually say anything.

Of course, the leader suggested another place we could go and continue praying. I seriously considered going into the bathroom on the way and staying there until the service started.

We went to the basement and circled up again, and a few more people joined us. There were about nine of us. This time, I could clearly hear everything people prayed. They took turns, praying for a few minutes at a time about the service and, I recall distinctly, about resurrection.

I held my breath.

And then my friend John prayed. He started praying about who God is. Honestly, I got even more nervous. But I listened attentively.

"God, your love is *relentless*."

The word echoed in my heart—not just for the following minutes but throughout the entire Easter service and then for hours, days, and weeks.

Relentless.

It would be a couple more months before I would pray over Gloria my first heartfelt, out loud prayer since Dad's death, but "the love of God and the void of God" were somehow held together in John's words. In that very moment, I actually noticed God's presence for the first time since Dad had died.

I was not forgotten. I was not unseen. God had not abandoned me.

God's primary response to suffering is *withness and witness*—the visible manifestation of God's presence in the midst of suffering.

———

The day after Dad died, Molly, my best friend since ninth grade, showed up at Jenna's house, where we were planning Dad's funeral.

Molly and I used to make up dances in each other's living rooms and work close to one another in our city's most popular shopping mall. On weeknights, when the mall was deserted, Molly would stand as far away from her jewelry kiosk as possible and I would stand as far away from the front of my sunglasses store as possible, and we would get paid to talk to one another.

I was relieved to find her at Jenna's front door.

Molly found me by contacting my mom. Right away, she explained that she came just to be there. She said she knew we had a lot to do. She brought her laptop and said she would be working near us, available if we needed her. Molly brought us food when it was time to eat, and she listened when we struggled with the outline for the funeral service. And she created space for stories about Dad.

It was so meaningful to be able to talk freely about him—to bring up every memory we could think of and laugh or cry.

Over the next two days, Molly offered no strategies for grief management. She did not invent reasons for why Dad died or try to fix us or stifle our emotions. She simply embodied God's love—her love—for us.

Witnessing to someone else's suffering and attending to it with deep listening is an essential part of holistic healing, healing through empathy that lessens the burden of suffering and its capacity to isolate the sufferer.

Most of Jesus's ministry was spent attending to people who were suffering. Jesus constantly recognized, embraced, listened to, and showed mercy to people who were suffering mentally, physically, socially, and existentially.

If there is anything that the stories about Jesus emphasize, it is that Jesus was a helper and healer of the wounded.

While talking with David Laws about the death of his daughter, Laura Hope, I asked him how he was supported in his time of grief. I wanted to know if there was anything that was particularly helpful.

David said that the day after learning about his daughter's death, he found himself at an AA meeting (he himself is sober and has been in long-term recovery) with two people next to him. David described a woman on his left and a man on his right who were witnesses to what he was going through, and he talked about how they shared similar life experiences and listened to one another.

I waited for him to go on, but he didn't.

That was it.

The most helpful thing for David Laws after his daughter died from an overdose was having people next to him who were also willing to be honest about their pain and wounds and who were willing to listen.

Near the end of my conversation with Lynn about Pookah, Charles, and Jazmine, I asked him what he thought people should be doing in light of increasing suicide rates. He was more specific than David, but what he told me was very similar.

"We need to recover the compassionate roots of pastoral care. We need to give individuals caring attention. We need churches that are *wholeness centered*, churches that engage voices of healing throughout the church, not just one voice," Lynn explained.

Months after the back-to-back funerals I experienced, my dear friend of nearly sixteen years, Chloe, became another witness to my pain. Chloe is the friend who bakes you cake from scratch on your birthday and makes sure you know how awesome she thinks you are. She was one of the first friends I made in Los Angeles.

Chapter 7

On a visit to California months after the deaths of my family members, Chloe and I went to the beach (she's also my swimming-in-the-ocean, diving-under-huge-waves companion), and for two hours in Los Angeles traffic I recounted my four weeks of hell to her.

It all suddenly came pouring out of me.

She knew the gist of what had happened, but for some reason in this moment I wanted to recall and reflect on every detail.

Chloe never interrupted me. She did not try to move the conversation along or change the subject. She did not try to relate my pain to her previous pain to connect with me. Chloe just listened for as long as I needed to speak.

When I asked Carli about how she was supported during her time of grief following the death of her sister, Madison, she described the immediate outpouring of kindness and support, and then she talked about the people who were with her and witnessed her pain long after the funeral:

> The one thing that really stuck out to me though was the help and support that was there months later. When you lose someone, especially so tragically and suddenly, so many people come out to show you they care. That usually goes away after a couple of weeks though and then the loneliness can start to set in. With Madison, I found it to be a similar situation, but there were some people who would still check in weeks, months and even years later now. That has meant so much. It shows that they also haven't forgotten about Madison and about what we must be going through. Showing up when everyone else has gone, that is what means the most to me

A couple of days after Dustin died, a small group of family members and I were shopping for funeral items when the group started discussing going to the place where Dustin had died by suicide. We were very close to the place, though I had not realized it.

I had no idea what to expect, and the day had already been filled with so much sorrow that I actually did not think I was capable of going. I was silently fearful of how it would feel to be there and how much it would hurt. But my family members imagined it would bring some comfort, and so we went.

It felt only right to say yes.

We drove through the entrance to a gravel parking lot. It was a cold day in December and the trees were bare. The parking lot was unoccupied. We found the spot where Dustin had parked his car, its lines still visible in the gravel. We parked our car next to the spot and got out.

I could hear the faint noise of cars driving by on the busy road near the entrance. The cold air filled my lungs. There was a line of giant trees behind us and a line of trees in front of us. Though it was the middle of winter, the place had a striking beauty to it.

Suddenly, I was consoled by the fact that Dustin died surrounded by these trees. And though the lot was empty and the place barren, I felt closer to Dustin there.

It was getting dark and the sun had almost set. As we were taking in the landscape we suddenly noticed a star above the trees. Standing next to each other in a line, we looked across the sky and one of us asked whether any other stars could be seen. There were none.

We realized that there was just this one exceedingly bright shining star in the sky.

Gazing at the star, we felt like Dustin met us there, that he allowed that single star to be seen in the sky so that we would know he was all right. It was not the kind of relief we wanted for him. It would have been far better for all of us and, I truly believe, for him if he had found peace another way.

But for a few minutes we allowed the tragedy of what had occurred in this very space just two days before to hang in the background and we instead focused on the star. And we all gave ourselves over to this moment. For the first time since Sunday morning we were not crying merely sad tears.

We were instead filled with a bright sorrow, a kind of transformative, quiet joy.

There is no deafening silence, imprisoned mind, or barren space that joy cannot break through. Because joy is God, because it is what you feel while being ministered to, it can always find you.

Exactly two years after Mason died, new life took her first breath.

Stef posted these words on one of her social media accounts: "Two years ago, January 2 had become a day I wanted to erase from my calendar forever. Fast forward to this year and my heart is filled with Joy that spills out of my eyes uncontrollably and it's all because this precious baby came today!"

Her stepson and his wife had their baby girl on this day.

In suffering, the longing for goodness and meaning is especially acute. In fact, we suffer because we are exceptionally attuned to the fact that what is good has died or is being obscured by that which is cruel and ruthless. In suffering, meaning is often eclipsed by seeming senselessness.

Since joy is "the present experience of God's being and becoming"—a recognition of God, the very manifestation of goodness and meaning—profound rejoicing is possible particularly in suffering.

Sometimes, observable signs of God's withness and love come in the form of stars or miraculous beginnings, like a baby just born.

Sometimes it is in dreams recalled a year later.

After booking the one-way ticket out of New Haven to try to see Dad before he passed away, I quickly packed. I threw a bunch of stuff into my green carry-on with very little thought. One of those things was my journal.

Before this trip I had never taken it anywhere outside my house because it contains so much information that is sacred and personal to me. I do not know why I grabbed it; in hindsight, I can only conclude that God put it in my mind to take it with me.

Because this miraculous action was such a gift to me a few days later.

I left New Haven to travel to see my dad on Thursday, January 19, 2017. Dad died in the middle of that night.

We planned his funeral for a few days later, Tuesday, January 24.

On the Sunday evening in between, I was trying to write my sermon for the funeral. I wanted to honor Dad by officiating the service, but I had no words. I was praying and asking God to help me. After sitting at Jenna's dining room table for a while trying to type, I suddenly remembered that I had brought my journal.

Unexpectedly, a vague memory of an entry where I recorded a conversation with my dad came to my mind.

I went upstairs and found the journal in my carry-on and flipped through its pages. I found an entry I'd written on January 24, 2016, what would be exactly one year before Dad's funeral.

On that day I had woken up and told Paul that I had a dream about Dad. I told Paul that I felt like God was telling me through the dream to call Dad and write down what he said. So I called my father and had a long, amazing conversation with him and wrote down much of what we discussed in this entry in my journal.

So I found myself in my sister's guest room two days before Dad's funeral reading words that Dad had said to me—strikingly, words like these: "When I die, don't cry, know I am in a better place."

In the midst of my deep sorrow, Dad's voice echoed in my ears as if he were sitting next to me. I realized the words we had shared nearly one year earlier were going to help me honor his life and faith at his very funeral.

During my brief sermon at the funeral, I told those present about the dream I had exactly one year earlier. I explained that I thought it appropriate to use my dad's own Bible during the service and to share some of his words from that beautiful conversation.

Dad always liked to have the last word anyway.

I also talked about Dad's underlined Bible, explaining that I did not know until I was given Dad's Bible just a few days earlier that throughout it he had often underlined the word "daughters."

For example, in the last chapter of the book of Job, where Job receives everything back again after he has experienced terrible grief and suffering, Dad underlined one verse, which reads, "And in all the land there were no women so fair as the daughters of Job."

The places where Dad underlined "daughters" in his Bible, as well as places he highlighted about God's presence, give me some consolation years later. I trust that in certain moments Dad felt true joy. I trust that there were moments in the last years of his life when he escaped his anxious thoughts, not with pills but instead with the comfort of a loving God who was with him and a witness to what he was going through.

I want to believe that Dad rejoiced over these moments and that, rather than avoiding his life, he fully embraced it in all its brutal and amazing glory.

During that phone conversation Dad had also said, "If you don't hear anything else from me, know I am proud of you." There they were, underlined in his Bible and written in my journal: precious reminders that my dad loved his daughters fiercely and was proud of them.

As we stumble through life, it is important to both lament openly the things that bring us pain *and* to search hard for beauty.

Just a day before writing this, I found a note from Dad sketched on yellow legal pad paper. I was packing boxes for our impending move to Texas because the Joy and the Good Life project grant had recently ended, and I was offered a new job at Truett Seminary at Baylor University.

Fittingly, in the note, Dad explained that he was sending me money and gave me instructions about my upcoming cross-country trip. When he wrote the note years earlier, I was about to head to Kentucky for the summer between my junior and senior years in college. He started the note with the words "Dearest Angela (My Little Messenger)."

The note admonished me to take regular breaks to exercise

and stretch. "And don't drive without at least two (2) or *more* nights' rest!" He closed the note writing, "May GOD continue to guide, bless, and keep you safe until we all see you on 5-15!!"

It brought me great joy to read his words again before taking another road trip, sixteen years later.

Reflecting back, instances of the inbreaking of joy and my decision to be receptive to this joy was essential for surviving the grief process, for being kept from despair, for nurturing genuine healing. Joy will always find us. But we have to be willing to give ourselves over to it.

Along with the note, I found pictures of Dad that I had not seen in a long time. One was of him and me having dinner.

In the photo, I had an eyebrow ring and apparently did not use sunscreen.

He was in a tie, the way I was used to.

In another photo Dad is sitting on a boat in the ocean. He is holding black sunglasses in one hand and pulling up his white ball cap with the other. His jet-black eyebrows are pointed up, and his hair and beard are messy from the ocean breeze. Dad is sticking his tongue out, making a silly face at the person taking the picture.

Textbook Dad.

And in another, Dad is posing in front of the New York City skyline, black-and-silver camcorder in hand.

I ended my sermon at Dad's funeral in the same way he ended our phone call exactly one year earlier. I wrote in my journal that he ended the call by saying, "I just love you. I love you very much."

I never understood or paid much attention to Holy Saturday before these tragedies happened. Now I think I know a bit more about what it means. Holy Saturday is the day between Jesus's death on Friday and his resurrection on Sunday morning.

It is the time *in between.*

It is the time spent somewhere between death on Friday and resurrection on Sunday, reconciling life's tremendous losses and unspeakable joys.

The majority of the time in our lives is spent living on Saturday, in the space between death on Friday and the indescribable joy of Sunday morning.

At multiple points during our lives, we find ourselves mourning death, carrying with us lament for places, ideas, relationships, experiences that are no more and for people who have died. After loss, we find ourselves desperate to make meaning of suffering, longing for resurrection, reunion, restoration.

Saturday is quiet.

We no longer hear the actual weeping of Friday evening, the shouts of rage, or the desperation of "My God, my God, why have you forsaken me?"

But death's sting is still palpable.

Since it is Saturday, others may not know that we have just attended a funeral or that our hearts are pounding with grief. Our tears are not flowing, so they do not see that we are suffering—that we have embraced goodbye, not yet, no, no more, the end.

Saturday is liminal space.

We know that we cannot possibly feel this way forever. We anticipate that we will see beauty, feel love, know hope, and find meaning again.

This is because we have known Sunday's goodness before, moments when our hearts pound instead with great joy, when unexpected and spontaneous connection, opportunity, renewal, and healing come.

Saturday is when we remember, we pray, we anticipate, we keep our hearts open.

On Saturday, we have not forgotten the horror of Friday but we also believe (Lord, help my unbelief) the sun will rise again.

Saturday is. Many of us must be here.

We stretch out our arms, one toward Friday and one toward Sunday. And when we do, perhaps, we will find one another's fingertips and maybe even discover Saturday is revealing something to us, perhaps even comforting us.

Maybe, possibly, Saturday will help us to see differently. *Though still through a mirror dimly.*

Of course, there will continue to be Friday evenings when we are in the thick of lament.

But there are surely more Sunday mornings to come when we will stumble onto the joy we long for and will be restored by it.

8

Stories to Tell

Love without anger and fear, never for-
get where I came from and where I was
headed.

—From the vision board of
one of the women in
the prison Bible study

Ezra is a somewhat short book in the Bible that few people reference because, quite frankly, it does not seem all that interesting at first glance. At one point, Ezra describes a bunch of people who are standing around watching the temple being rebuilt.

See what I mean?

Yes, they are watching something be reconstructed. A version of watching paint dry.

But Ezra makes an observation about this moment that captured my attention one morning the way the word "relentless" had in John's prayer.

Ezra writes that some of the people watching are shouting praises excitedly because the foundation has just been laid for the new building. But other people are weeping loudly when they see the foundation because they can remember the old house. Ezra explains that there was so much noise that it was difficult to distinguish the sound of the joyful shouts from the sound of the weeping.

I remember meditating on the idea of sounds of rejoicing and sounds of weeping happening all at once. I read the passage over and over again, realizing it consoled me. I felt safer about the mere idea of allowing joy in, knowing joy can be expressed in such close proximity to sorrow.

As I reflected on my life I realized I knew what Ezra was talking about, even and especially during my family's weeks of hell.

———

After Mason's sudden death, my sisters and I sat on stools around Stef's kitchen counter for three days straight, leaving only a few times: once to pick up takeout, once to buy an urn, and once to attend Mason's funeral.

Perhaps it was our version of *sitting shiva.*

Chapter 8

We sat around the counter eating, drinking wine (except for Jenna, who was pregnant), telling stories, crying, laughing, and likely trying to make sense of Mason's death even though we all know there is no actual way to make sense of a young person's death.

Jenna's pregnancy was embodied hope on those bleak days in Albuquerque. She was carrying a baby that we had been praying for. Somehow looking at the ultrasound photos that she had brought with her made that dark time pregnant with possibility.

She could not contain her joy—even as it was tinged with the sorrow—as she looked lovingly at those photos. And neither could we.

One moment we were talking about being disoriented by the previous weeks, mystified by the mere idea that Mason was no longer alive, and the next we were guessing this baby's gender—*seized by joy.*

This baby was going to be the boy, Ro, with Dad's fierce, black eyebrows, the baby that, unbeknownst to us, Jenna would be telling Dad about just a week later, while he was dying in the hospital room.

Joy is a counteragent to despair because it can be sustained and sustain us, even when standing right next to sorrow.

At one point, we told Stef she needed her favorite foods—tortilla chips, guacamole, and salsa. We told her we were going to go to one of her preferred local spots to get takeout for her.

I have learned that when someone is facing a crisis, they do not need questions like, "What can we do to help?" or empty offers like, "Let me know if you need anything."

They need you to bring them food and chocolate and fuzzy socks to wear. They need you to clean their bathroom and clean out their refrigerator. They need you to sit next to them and listen to their memories and witness their tears. They need you to share silence with them, too.

And then they need to know it is okay for them to laugh. Loudly.

We placed the food in the middle of our circle, and we talked about the past—the other times we had eaten these same foods together.

Salsa, guacamole, and tortilla chips were our balms of Gilead.

Sometimes the conversation around the counter became light and fun. We talked about how Dad sent all of us to Vacation Bible School when we were little. We discussed the songs they taught us there.

Suddenly, one of my sisters belted out this song: "I am a C, I am a C-H, I am a C-H-R-I-S-T-I-A-N, and I have C-H-R-I-S-T in my H-E-A-R-T and I will -L-I-V-E in . . ." and before we knew it, we were all loudly clapping our hands and singing along at the top of our lungs.

We had probably not sung the song in over twenty-five years, but we could all remember the words. We laughed boisterously, surprised at what had just happened. We all agreed that Dad bringing us together and helping ensure that we knew about God's love were two of the best things he ever did.

Joy is not dependent on sorrow, but joy can accompany sorrow. My sisters and I were able to rejoice and laugh together around the counter while we mourned Mason's death.

To recognize and embrace joy is not to neglect telling the truth about what is happening.

Joy is not naive.

———————

During a recent worship service I was especially sad about Dad. After the service, I struggled to engage in conversation with people around me, distracted by my grief.

Suddenly, I heard giggling.

I looked around the room to see where it was coming from. Two little girls were riding on the feet of a man with black hair who was taking giant steps around the room.

Most of us know what it is to see something but then to *see something else* entirely in our mind's eye.

Joy is excess—meaning beyond meaning.

At that moment I did not just see the two little girls and the man in front of me. I saw Jenna and Dad and me, too. I saw the relationships we had and the fun they had nurtured. As I gazed at these three playing together, I saw my past and their present connect, and I marveled at the moment as it filled me with a reverent, grateful joy.

Joy is a feeling that "often accompanies a realization of our relatedness." Anguish often follows aloneness, but joy often follows *relatedness.*

You can substitute lots of words for "relatedness," for instance, "kinship," "harmony," and "significance." Relatedness lessens misery, and the joy that accompanies such a realization of connection counteracts despair. In the place of distance, despondency, and hopelessness, joy brings a sudden sense of belonging, understanding, and significance.

A realization of relatedness—to a person, purpose, experience, story, value, object, or nature—can happen at any moment. And we can pray for and seek such realizations too.

We can meditate on things that point beyond themselves, things that are all around us: "music, the birth of a baby, the appearance of spring flowers, grass growing through the concrete, and the irrepressibility of human love."

I've learned that when we do such meditating, we begin to see things as more significant than we might have first imagined, not just other people but anything, even everyday objects.

When my sister Stefanie looks at a mason jar, she does not see just a jar. She sees her son. She hears his voice, remembers his texts, recalls the video games he loved, and hears the song she often sang to him play in her head:

"You are my sunshine, my only sunshine. You make me happy when skies are gray. You'll never know, dear, how much I love you. Please don't take my sunshine away."

Whenever Stef sees a mason jar, she sees a Mason jar—whether in someone's hand filled with tea or bursting with flowers on a friend's coffee table. And because it is not just an object she is seeing, but a relationship imbued with beauty, goodness, and meaning, she is then filled with an indescribable joy.

Joy is an illumination, the ability to see beyond to *something more*.

Eventually, the practice of looking beyond, of searching for *the something more* that touches so many aspects of life, helps us to recognize the permeability of our lives and the fact that we are not as alone as we may feel. It helps us to recognize that life is not as empty, bleak, or worthless as we were beginning to think.

———

Nina Lau-Branson, a spiritual director, coach, and group facilitator who lives in Southern California, had an idea. Nina knew people who oversaw transition houses for people coming out of prison and rehabilitation in her community.

Nina's idea was to have regular, voluntary groups, called Council, with these residents.

Nina has been trained in the Center for Council's "age-old practice that involves bringing people together in a circle to bear witness and share authentically."

At first, the leadership of the transition houses was hesitant. The members are already required to go to Alcoholics Anonymous meetings.

But Nina insisted that Council was different. Nina told the leadership that leading Council circles would nurture space for the residents to reflect on their experiences—not just related to addiction but also about many aspects of their lives. Nina believed the practices of Council could add to the residents' healing journeys. Nina asked the leadership to give her the opportunity to simply experiment and see what happened.

Ultimately, they agreed to let her experiment. And Nina was willing to share with me what has happened.

The design is quite simple. Everyone is invited to tell and

listen to stories, speaking and listening from the heart in a nonjudgmental way.

Nina started with one men's group and one women's group. Each time she meets with the residents, she does the same thing. When she first starts meeting with a group, she often personally sets an intention for the session, something like "build joy and create spaces for laughter." The group members don't know what her intention is, but she believes they feel it.

Council is about intention rather than technique.

The overall intention of speaking and listening from the heart and the act of setting an intention for each gathering are what make Council circles unique.

Nina starts each circle time by inviting participants to play a game with each other.

After this, each person makes a dedication. They dedicate the session to whomever or whatever they want. This is a meaningful part of Council too. There are few spaces like this where people intentionally dedicate time to someone or something.

This simple act suddenly gives significance to their time together and invites residents to recognize that this time is sacred, worthy, and meaningful.

Perhaps many of us need more opportunities to do activities for the sake of something beyond ourselves.

As Nina listens to the dedications, she tries to discern a common thread in what the group members are sharing. One night, the women's dedications were all related to people in the women's lives who had helped them in some way, so Nina invited the women who wanted to do so to tell a story about someone in their life who had helped them.

Similarly, during a particularly meaningful night in the men's group, Nina asked the men to describe a time when they needed help and that help arrived.

If someone does not want to share, Nina says something like, "We will hold stories in silence too, recognizing there is still a story there even if someone does not speak it aloud."

After everyone who wanted to share has done so, Nina leads a "witness round" where group members share things like, "I heard someone say . . ." in order to show people they were heard.

Nina's Council groups embody withness and witness.

Nina has heard powerful things from men and women who have been a part of the groups. Things like, "You've given me back my life."

"I have remembered things that I had long forgotten."

"There were people who really loved me."

Reflections like these are forms of healthy relief and comfort in the midst of pain. Not only this, but there is joy in finding what has been lost. There is joy in remembering the good that has happened to us and been given to us.

Like Nina's groups, we need to find ways to offer each other the chance to reimagine and enjoy experiences of grace, strength, goodness, beauty, and love.

Together, we can recall to mind joyful experiences—moments when we have witnessed goodness, when someone told us life-giving truth, when someone helped us in our time of need or loved us unconditionally. Together, as Nina's Council circles do, we can try to make such memories as vivid as possible and give them heightened attention, which can help us to feel joy in the moments following this remembering, even if the memory is someone else's.

This kind of remembering and imagining counteracts sources of pain—perceived failure, inadequacy, shame—that can feed despair.

Nina believes that over time the group members have realized that *everyone has a story*, even themselves. Nina says, "It's something we all share. Just some of us are more practiced at telling our story."

Storytelling can reconnect us with the truths, the goodness, the beauty, and the meaning that we have witnessed in our lives. Telling our stories also nurtures empathy and understanding between people, forms of connection that can elicit joy.

The men and women in Nina's groups have told her that Council circles have made an incredible difference because they are about remembering who they are as human beings.

Chapter 8

"The residents of the transitional houses are rediscovering their humanity—that we all have things to celebrate. We all have fears. We have all experienced suffering. We all desire to matter. We all want to feel connected," Nina explained.

Members of both men's and women's groups are rediscovering what it means to be faithfully present with other people and to be fully honest, as I rediscovered in the prison Bible study.

Council circles have even led the residents to form a community beyond their sessions with Nina. For example, people are now frequently gathering together in a common space in the men's residence that was not previously being used. There have been spontaneous barbecues and parties to watch sports together.

"Recently, there was a yard sale and the men were welcoming and talking with their neighbors, something that had not happened at past neighborhood events," Nina said.

They have become a community that is drawing others into community.

Nina has great hopes for these circles. While people tell their stories, she wants group members to know that they are seen. And she wants them to know that the group is going to tell the truth about them and hold them in love.

Council circles are a simple idea in design, but they are a radical practice today.

These circles embody what many of us are deeply longing for, moments where we feel seen and heard and where we tell the truth—places to talk about what has happened to us, spaces to remember goodness and find meaning—making room to nurture a positive sense of self, honesty, and hope.

Human beings, young and old, have two bedrock needs: belonging and effectiveness. In fact, suicidal thinking often occurs when people experience loneliness and feel like they have become a burden or ineffective. The collision of these feelings can be detrimental. Nina's circles are meeting fundamental human needs that make life worth living—people are discovering that they are a part of a community and that their life has significance.

Despair struggles to breathe where meaning resides.

Like Nina's Council circles, we need to pick up (or pick up

again) the practices of storytelling and testifying that have been vibrant activities in both Latinx and Black communities.

Cultural memory, as described by Christian educator Anne Streaty Wimberly, is "memory within a particular, cultural group that has in it, images, knowledge, visions, values, poetry, music and so on that builds the identity of a culture," and cultural memory is connected to joy because "embedded in each one of those is a sense of joy or how we feel about what has happened in the lives of a people, but also how we have come through difficulties."

Describing through stories how people we know—family or chosen family, and neighbors—have situated their suffering in the larger context of life or even made meaning from suffering also inspires hope and encourages us to do the same.

Similarly, stories where love prevails and joy was felt can both give us a picture (a model) of what love and joy look like as well as nurture positive expectations for the future. We can imagine that such love and joy are possible in our lives too.

Plus, if we learn to see ourselves as people who are continuing a narrative that many other people before us have carried and embodied, we can imagine our present and future as shared.

Religious education professor Almeda Wright talks about the importance of inviting young people in particular "to be a part of this cultural memory, to see themselves as part of a continuation of the memory, a continuation of this story . . . [so they can] be able to say this is my story too."

In other words, telling stories about communal suffering helps us to remember that we can view the overcoming of suffering as a communal task rather than as a task we must pursue alone.

Suddenly your stories—your experiences of overcoming suffering or encountering and embodying love, hope, and joy—are mine too. We can sense that the goodness, significance, and truths of the past are passed on to us.

The meaning of my life is caught up in the meaning of the community.

We need people who both tell us stories and help us to realize that we too have stories to tell.

When I asked Nina why she believed more of us do not do this kind of thing—invite people to share their stories, speaking and listening from the heart—she said, "We cannot facilitate or give away what we do not have."

One of my favorite people is a Roman Catholic nun named Suzanne. She was in her early seventies when we first met, so she had been keeping her vows for nearly fifty years at that point. She also has a PhD in psychology and years of experience in spiritual direction and leading a parish.

I immediately connected with her during our first encounter.

When I lived in Los Angeles I went to see Suzanne regularly. The night before going to see her was like Christmas Eve for me. I looked forward to our conversations with great anticipation. I realize now that part of the reason I got so much out of our talks was because I imagined they were going to be important.

There is something to this kind of imagining—to being ready for time spent with someone to be significant, to being prepared to find joy.

Whenever I pulled into my parking spot near Suzanne's house, my heart warmed and my soul settled. I knew she was going to share her wisdom with me. I knew her presence and soothing words would offer me healing and insight, which were integrally tied to one another.

I knew which house was hers—even though the neighborhood has a bunch of houses that look similar—because hers has a white, three-foot stone statue of Mary out front. It's interesting now to reflect on Mary being out front to greet me. Mary was a poor teenager when God came to her and asked if she wanted to be the mother of Jesus. With great joy she accepted the task—rejoicing that God saw her.

Suzanne always greeted me on her covered porch with a hug. She would sit in her recliner, and I would sit on her couch. I talked about anything and everything, and she listened attentively.

Sometimes she would chime in and offer me a new way of thinking about something I had just said. Other times she waited until the very last minutes of our conversation, and she would then point me to a book she thought I needed to read or teach me a new spiritual practice.

Often, she asked me questions that helped me to reframe what was happening in my life, questions that would help me to consider God's invitations in my experiences. For example, once she asked, "What might God be teaching you in the waiting?"

No matter what she said, Suzanne always looked at me in a way that made me believe she really saw me, heard me, and believed me.

The only way any of us learns to be present to others, to see one another truly, to tell our stories, and to ask important questions that help us get from one experience in life to the next is precisely this—learning by watching.

Someone has to teach us. Someone has to see us. Someone has to model attentive, deep listening. Someone has to show us how to be present with other people in compassionate, loving ways. Someone has to help us learn which questions to ask and guide us in genuine discernment.

Everyone I tell about Suzanne wants to sit on her porch too.

It seems the kind of conversations Suzanne and I had on her porch for four years are the kinds of conversations we all long to have. We want guidance. We long for help hearing God's voice. We want space to share what has happened to us. And we want to be seen, heard, and believed.

"A Christian community is therefore a healing community not because wounds are cured and pains are alleviated, but because wounds and pains become openings or occasions for a new vision," writes author Henri Nouwen.

That's what Suzanne did for me. She always helped me to see my life and its pain with perspective and to look for God's invitations and responses in the midst of life's disruptions—good and bad.

I never felt like a disappointment or a failure when talking to Suzanne. It was just not possible because she allowed me to share how I had disappointed myself or others, ways I had failed, *without shame.*

Spaces where we can freely speak without any worry, without any shame, are healing spaces that powerfully offset the other spaces in our lives where we hide what we really think, what really happened, and what we are truly feeling.

Madison's sister, Carli, believes that expressing empathy in the way Suzanne always has for me is the most powerful way to help when someone is having suicidal thoughts.

Carli said, "If empathy is what can erase shame, I think it is what can erase suicide as well."

Around Suzanne, it was impossible to imagine that life was purely disappointment or failure. She always made me believe my pain could be transformed.

Nouwen also said that "when we become aware that we do not have to escape our pains, but that we can mobilize them into *a common search for life,* those very pains are transformed from expressions of despair into signs of hope."

A college student whom I heard recently, Treasure Ramirez, described something similar. She talked about people in her life who have helped her turn her "wounds into wisdom."

Given Suzanne's uncanny ability to always help me search for life and turn my wounds into wisdom, Suzanne was one of the first people I wanted to see after the weeks of hell. Since I had moved to Connecticut, I had to wait until I had a break from work to fly back and see her (as well as my best friends in Los Angeles whom I desperately needed to share a meal with and cry with).

As I parked near her house (my dear friend Katie let me borrow her car), just like all those times before, my heart expanded with great expectation.

I sat down on her couch and told her every detail of those horrifying weeks.

As Suzanne listened, she embodied incredible compassion. And at the end she lovingly and honestly said, "Every time someone close to us dies, a part of us dies with them. This is painful. It also leaves room for forms of new life to spring up in us."

It would be a long time before I would know exactly what she meant.

———

Similar to the question about how pain fits into a good life, the question Jayla asked the Bible study group the night she told us about her suicide attempt is also one we must all strive to answer.

What is there to live for?

"Despair seems to close down the future," writes theologian James Cone. Joy, on the other hand, as priest Justin Crisp explains, "casts a positive vision for what life is truly *for.*"

Whereas apathy is a result of not caring and not being concerned with one's position or condition in the world, passionate concern and its effect—joy—are the opposite of apathy.

People who are incarcerated, Ivy League students, and you and I—all human beings—have in common the quest of discerning and verbalizing a life worth living. We need a way of life that provides meaning and so we must search for it.

During the course of the Wednesday night Bible study gatherings at the prison, we moved from questions like, "What is your deepest longing?," to even deeper questions like, "What is *worth* wanting?" What human beings desperately need, says author Viktor Frankl, is "the striving and struggling for a worthwhile goal."

One evening, I brought white paper and markers to Bible study for what I called "vision boards." I invited the women to use the markers to draw or put words on the paper that represented the vision they had for their lives. I asked them to consider what should be important to them and to describe what is worth living for.

They wasted no time. They grabbed the paper and the markers and took places all over the room and began drawing and writing.

After they made the boards, we hung them around the room, and I asked if anyone wanted to talk about their board. Each one of the pieces of paper revealed beautiful, articulate hopes.

Lee talked about working at night and going to school during the day so that she could become a drug and alcohol counselor.

Tonya described the importance of gaining strength, peace, self-worth, honesty, and the ability to let God love her.

Gabrielle said she wanted to live a life of "no shame, self-love, love for others."

Conversations about life's most important questions provide opportunities for communities like ours at the prison Bible study and in the Life Worth Living courses to talk about how we find fulfillment and realize our relatedness in life beyond work.

People in genuine communities help one another to consider conceptions of vocation that include other areas of life. In community we can discern where we can find connection, and what we might commit ourselves to, as individuals and as a community.

If we can be fulfilled by our work, if we find a job that we love, there is certainly joy in this. However, if we work at jobs solely to pay our bills, there are plenty of other ways to find coherence and to feel like what we are doing aligns with our values, is meaningful to us and others, and ultimately matters. In other words, there are many ways beyond work to realize meaning and feel joy. But we need visions of the good life that are not only or even primarily tied to money (and other insubstantial conceptions).

We need worthier desires.

In a talk called "Why the Pursuit of Happiness Is a Bad Idea," Jennifer Herdt, professor of Christian ethics, describes how seeking to engage in pursuits that are truly worthwhile, as opposed to desiring happiness, transforms what we desire.

Herdt puts it this way: "Seeking to live life well *does* mean renouncing your own happiness, your own life-satisfaction, as a final end in itself, as a goal worth allowing to govern and structure your pursuits. But it does *not* mean a life of stern duty and self-denial, a life of squelching your desires and passions. For as you take up the task of living well, seeking to engage in pursuits that are truly worthwhile, your desires are transformed."

Herdt gives the example of "the vegetarian who now dislikes the taste of meat, or the couch potato turned marathon runner who can't stand to go a day without a run," explaining "our tastes change as we develop new dispositions, new ways of seeing and experiencing the world." In fact, "your perception of what is *truly good and worthy of devotion* is also transformed in the process of its pursuit," Herdt explains.

At the end of the night, after the women exited the room, I gazed at the visions hanging on the wall.

The words on one sign were simple to say, but hard to do: "Stay prayed up!"

One person wrote, "Not just a person from the projects who dies without changing the world, even if it is something as small as the ripple effect." She drew blue ripples of water around the words.

Another vision board had several concrete aspirations that together demonstrated not just what sort of life would be worth living but how she might get there too, "Recovery, God #1, trauma therapist, motivational speaker, work with inner-city children."

Another woman declared that she wanted "to make her family proud, be a devoted wife, find a job helping people and be joyful and spiritually attuned."

I stared at one sign for several minutes. It read, "Love without anger and fear, never forget where I came from and where I was headed."

We do not often take time to name out loud our fundamental values, but this is important work because our values are deeply connected with what we do with our time and how we develop as people. When you feel that the way you live corresponds with, affirms, and embodies your goals and values, you often feel joy.

About five weeks after Amy attempted suicide, she walked into Bible study. It took every ounce of restraint I had not to reach out my arms and grab her and hug her tight. I got close to

Amy's face and looked into her eyes and tried to hug her with my own.

I tried to convey to her what Jordan had said and how we had all prayed for her that night and begged God for her to feel our love through the prison walls.

Amy came to Bible study on vision board night too.

In the midst of Amy's struggle to recover from the trauma of her past, to forgive and love herself, all while living in a prison, she began to have a vision for life; and that vision, importantly, accounts for suffering.

She raised her hand and, after being invited to share, Amy bluntly said she wanted to wipe people's butts in a nursing home one day. The way she said it was funny, but no one laughed because she was incredibly excited and serious about it.

Amy went on to lovingly explain that people had cared for her and she didn't mind caring for others—especially those who really need help like older people in nursing homes who often are forgotten. She said she knew what it was to feel forgotten.

Amy and the other women at the Bible study showed me that what does not kill you can make you more empathetic.

Amy rejoiced over her vision board because we rejoice over those things that remind us of who we most deeply and truly are and those things that facilitate becoming the people that we know we most deeply and truly are.

The visions that were shared revealed a value for independence but also for interdependence. When the women shared their visions, they addressed the past and they imagined engaging life rather than avoiding it, as so many of them had used substances to do. Many of them articulated their goals and values in terms of staying focused on God and discovering a sense of self and meaning in God's love.

When God's love is understood as the foundation of everything, we can look for God's love in all people, in every place, in each moment. The sense that God's love is identifiable, reachable—closer than my breath and ever-present—has given me profound comfort and a continued awareness that meaning, truth, beauty, and goodness persist even and especially in sheer silence.

"Silence is the language of God," says Suzanne.

As painful as it can be, when the world is quiet, we can hear more clearly and see more truthfully. In silence, we are awakened. We realize we are breathing, hungry, desiring, which causes us to seek. To seek is to simultaneously resist becoming numb. In silence, we relearn how to listen, how to reach out, how to welcome something other than our own words, feelings, and ideas.

In silence, God miraculously helped me to become more like Amy, to sit on the edge of the seat of my own life again, curious, eager, receptive.

Once we are able to answer questions like, "How does pain fit into a good life?" and "What is worth living for?," we also need to be able to answer questions like, "What happens if we fail?"

I have come to realize it was extremely important for students in Life Worth Living and women in the prison Bible study and for me with Suzanne to talk together about how to deal with disappointment, mistakes, and failure, because these things are inevitable.

We will not always live up to the visions that we or others have for our lives.

We will fail sometimes.

So we have to anticipate disappointment, mistakes, and failure and be committed to revealing these things rather than hiding them. Often this also means being willing to apologize and forgive. It means courageously confronting disappointment, mistakes, and failure, and seeking healing from them.

⎯⎯⎯⎯

When my stepbrother, James, married Michelle, I knew she was a gem of a human being. Michelle is confident and driven in a way that inspires you. She is kind and easy to be around. She really looks at you when you're talking, something that is striking in a society where so few people seem to be really interested in what other people are saying.

Chapter 8

One day, while writing this book, I recalled that I had heard Michelle say at her wedding reception, during her nonalcoholic toast of gratitude to the crowd, something about having a past related to substances.

So I decided to text Michelle and asked if she wanted to email me a bit of her story and talk about what gave her hope and what continues to nurture that hope. I ended with, "No pressure, just thought I'd ask."

True to Michelle's character she wrote, "I would love to chat with you on video. It's easier for me to express my emotions and convey my feelings when I can see you."

So we set a time and date.

A couple of weeks later, as we ended the video chat in which she told me some of her story, I marveled at how much I had learned. Truly, I was astonished at how little I actually knew about Michelle's life.

I should not have been surprised, though. Before this I had never asked if she had a story to tell.

Michelle talked about her mother being Chinese and her father being white. Like Lynn's cousin, Jazmine, growing up with two identities was difficult for her. Sometimes comments were made about her identity that made accepting herself especially hard.

"I was always insecure," Michelle said. "I wanted to be accepted and noticed. I was awkward," she recalled.

So as a young teenager, when her cousin (who was much older than she was) and her cousin's friends accepted her into their friend group and welcomed her into their communal experiences of drug use, she felt something she had longed for.

She belonged.

This sense of belonging became especially important once her parents began to constantly argue (they would eventually get a divorce) and she began homeschooling herself. Since she was not attending a school with peers, was working, did not really have extracurricular activities, and did not go to church, the friends she did drugs with were her only companions.

One day, the group was doing meth together, so Michelle tried it. She recalled, "I stayed up for three days straight, and it gripped me like nothing else had. After that, it was all I wanted."

Michelle began spending all of the money she had saved and worked for on drugs.

She loved meth but also needed Xanax to be able to calm down and sleep. She constantly went back and forth between using all kinds of uppers and downers, a pattern that many people abusing substances know well. Often this is the only way people who are addicted to substances make it through any given day and the only way they eventually get to sleep.

Like many people who become addicted to a substance like meth, Michelle realized she could no longer support her habit by working at a conventional job, so she started selling meth. "The setup was perfect. I had an endless supply of the drug I loved and lots of money to keep using it and pay my rent," she explained.

However, on Michelle's nineteenth birthday, she suddenly decided she could not keep selling and using. What had begun as a sincere feeling of connection with others had turned into a nightmare. She realized her life had become chaotic and unmanageable.

Out of nowhere, with simply her willpower, Michelle stopped using, started going to college, and stayed clean for several months.

But then something happened that dramatically changed the course of her life. This one development and what occurred afterward would radically influence the way she saw herself for years to come.

Michelle discovered she was pregnant.

At nineteen and newly sober, Michelle did not feel like she could raise a child because she could barely take care of herself. She struggled with the very idea of bringing another person, an innocent person, into the difficult circumstances of her life.

In the haze of immense stress, she terminated her pregnancy.

With wet eyes and pain that was palpable so many years later, Michelle said, "My abortion felt like a giant secret, a terrible thing I had done that I could not talk to anyone about."

Afterward, Michelle was deeply troubled with regret and remorse. She said that her abortion caused her to believe that in the core of her being she was a bad person.

I realized that Michelle had lived with immense shame for years, shame that she could not share with anyone, shame that she had previously imagined could never be redeemed.

Michelle started dabbling with meth again.

For the next few years, whenever she needed relief from her secret, her regret, and her belief that she was a bad person, she self-medicated with substances.

"Secrets keep you sick," Michelle said.

I knew immediately that I would meditate on this one sentence for a long time.

———

At twenty-two, Michelle ran into an old friend who saw that she was depressed.

"My friend took me to a strip club to cheer me up," Michelle said.

As I listened to Michelle tell her story, it became apparent that detrimental sources of relief and escape kept piling on top of one another. Small acts of desperation for comfort snowball quickly.

That evening at the strip club would shape the next few years of Michelle's life in significant ways.

She met Luke, who had just been released from prison. He was put in prison for trafficking the drug Michelle loved most, meth.

Luke started frequently staying with Michelle, and just two months after they met, Michelle got pregnant again. This time with twins.

Once she found out she was pregnant, Michelle immediately decided to stop using alcohol and meth. At this point she was working for her dad's company, and so she helped Luke to get a job there too.

Luke and Michelle even got engaged.

It seemed her life was finally headed in the right direction and things were coming together. Michelle was doing her best to keep her life in order and was staying sober. But one day, one of the babies died in her womb.

Michelle was completely devastated.

Since she still had another baby living inside of her, though, she continued to stay sober and tried to maintain hope during the profoundly difficult weeks afterward.

Then, during a doctor's appointment, at twenty-three weeks and two days pregnant, Michelle was told that the other baby had serious health issues and likely would not live until birth. And if the baby lived through birth the illness would almost guarantee the baby would not live to be a year old.

The information was shocking; the grief was overwhelming.

The doctor told Michelle she could terminate her pregnancy only at twenty-four weeks or less, which meant she only had four days to make the hardest decision she had ever had to make.

"I was distraught because I really wanted this baby and Luke had proposed, and everything seemed to be working out. I could not imagine having another abortion. At the same time, I was not doing well having had the other baby die in my womb just weeks before. I did not think I could emotionally or mentally handle having a stillborn baby or finding a baby dead in their crib," she recalled, crying all these years later.

After four days of crying and sheer anguish, Michelle's mom and Luke went with her to the doctor to terminate the pregnancy.

Michelle described weeping on the table.

"Afterward, I asked for a prescription for Xanax, and the doctor gave it to me. I was very close to taking the entire bottle. I didn't know how to deal with the pain. And I did not feel that anyone could understand my pain."

A few weeks later a friend brought her the kind of respite

she was familiar with. She used cocaine because "any relief was welcome at that point and it numbed the pain."

All over again, the cycle of uppers and downers repeated.

And not just in her life, but in Luke's life, too. They got married, but their relationship was centered around drug and alcohol use.

Eventually, they began having arguments based on drinking and drugs, and then Luke started cheating on her.

One night, while she was asleep, Luke came home drunk.

Michelle got out of bed to confront him about waking her up. She saw he was on his phone. She grabbed it and found explicit texts on it from another woman.

"I slapped him, and a look of pure evil came across his face," she said.

Though Michelle was only wearing a tee shirt and underwear and it was the middle of the night, she ran to her sister's house close by.

Luke ran after her and as she was pounding on her sister's door screaming for help, Luke caught up to her and began to beat her on her sister's porch, punching her in the face. He grabbed her by her hair and dragged her down the concrete steps until the skin on her legs and arms became raw.

"My sister finally opened the front door, and I crawled toward her with blood all over my face," Michelle said.

She pressed charges, and since Luke was still on parole he went back to prison. Michelle filed for divorce.

Michelle moved in with her sister and tried once again to get her life back. For years, Michelle would try to stop using substances and then incredibly painful things would happen; she would feel desperate for relief and start using again, with no ability to imagine any other way to work through her pain.

She was doing all right until she reconnected with a guy

named Kato, someone from her old drug circle who had something—someone really—that she had been longing for.

Kato had a child. Kato's baby fulfilled her for a while and seemingly filled the holes left in her heart after her babies had died.

Kato and Michelle got involved in a committed relationship,
and she became pregnant again, something she truly wanted.

Kato remained a drug user and a drug dealer, which led him
to prison while she was pregnant. Despite the drugs in her house
and Kato going to prison, Michelle stayed sober during her entire
pregnancy, desperate to protect this baby.

When Kato went to prison she wanted connection again.
"I was lonely and afraid of having a baby alone."

So even though he had tried to kill her, Luke was invited back
into Michelle's life.

"He had a hold on me for so long," Michelle said. She talked
about him the way she talked about meth.

"Luke was respected by people in the drug world. People
wanted to be him. It helped me to deal with my insecurities because I got recognition from being with him. He was strong and
protective," she explained.

Michelle was especially drawn to Luke because of the way he
supported her during her pregnancy and during the birth of her
daughter, Kylen.

"Luke actually fed Kylen her first bottle and helped to give Kylen
her first bath. He really seemed to love her," Michelle reflected.

However, true to form, the sweetness and joy did not last.
Luke started using meth again and then heroin. And six weeks
after Kylen was born, Michelle found herself lying on the bathroom floor, exhausted, with post-partum depression. While she
was grateful for Kylen, she began having suicidal thoughts again.
So she self-medicated the only way she knew how.

"Since Luke was using and selling again, I had an endless supply of meth and Xanax to turn to."

After a short time, Luke got busted again and went back to
jail. And again, Michelle found herself alone, with the man she
had been doing life with in prison.

This time, Michelle was especially fearful because there were a lot of people Luke owed money to, which meant there were people she owed money to.

She found herself once more abusing substances, this time in desperate need of protection and connection.

When she met Carter, she realized he solved a bunch of her problems at once. He used alcohol and meth and had a direct line to a drug cartel. He gave her access to every type of drug she had ever loved. He helped her financially—he actually paid back people on Luke's behalf. And he had a place where she could live.

Carter became her best friend and, eventually, her boyfriend.

Michelle describes this time with Carter as "the most stability I had in a long time."

To do her part, Michelle began selling drugs with Carter (and to her own horror years later) took Kylen along. She is shocked at her own behavior.

Michelle reflected, "I do not understand how this made sense to me at the time. Eventually, someone called Child Protective Services and Kylen was taken away from me and placed with my mom. After losing Kylen, my drug use spiraled out of control."

She stayed up for days and weeks at a time. Michelle was introduced to a new drug, GHB, and "life became a 24-7 party." Often, they would go to hotels to meet suppliers.

"One night, we were sitting in a hotel room surrounded by drugs, and five Federal agents raided our hotel room." Michelle remembers one of the agents asking, "What are you doing with your life?"

That moment has stayed with her.

What happened next is pretty wild.

"Carter was able to cut a deal with the feds. He agreed to work with them, but only if they would not charge me. Since they wanted the suppliers above him the feds took the deal. They let me walk free."

I took a deep breath as I continued to listen and take notes.

They went back to Carter's house, and the reality of what had happened and what Carter was facing hit them. "We cried and held each other because Carter knew his life was over, and we knew we would eventually be separated," Michelle said.

And it was true.

For Carter, the raid in the hotel room was the beginning of the end.

"Carter had to set people up so they could be busted for drug trafficking and it weighed heavy on him. He saw himself as a big rat who was bringing down people. He became extremely depressed."

On a day that Michelle remembers vividly, Carter broke a bunch of stuff in the house and texted her, writing, "I can't do this. I'm killing myself."

She was in another part of the house.

She could hear a ladder scooting across the garage floor. Carter locked the doors and texted that he didn't want her to see it. Michelle called her mom and asked her to dial 911.

Carter was miraculously rescued in time and taken by police to the hospital.

"Everything became too much, and we split up with each other," she explained.

Each time tragedy struck, the only thing that Michelle felt could pull her from depression and give her the relief she needed was drug use and selling drugs.

So she did the one thing she knew to do to find the relief she longed for.

She reconnected with a person from her older cousin's friend circle, the person who first introduced to her meth when she was sixteen. She began using meth again.

"He did not know that I had been raided by federal agents.

No one but Carter did. So one day he dropped by my house to give me a half ounce of meth. The street value was $2,400. He gave it to me, and said, 'Get yourself out of bed. You know what to do.'"

Michelle contacted everyone she knew and suddenly had tons of people selling for her. Michelle and her team sold heroin, cocaine, meth, and pills.

She began partying and enjoying the grand life of being one of the most well-liked drug dealers in town.

A little too well-liked.

One day, someone got pulled over after buying drugs at her house. The police found the drugs in his car and threatened to tell his family about his drug use. But they were willing to let him go if he would tell them where he bought the drugs.

Police started watching her house.

Between the flow of people and the drugs, Michelle felt like she had power. She explained, "I felt like I had a business. People wanted to hang out with me. I was the girl everyone wanted to know. I was finally popular."

Everything she longed for came together for Michelle in using and selling substances.

Relief from shame and depression and pain.

Happiness and a life she could enjoy.

Belonging. Identity. Purpose.

After getting a new supply of drugs and pulling into her driveway one night, Michelle got out of her car and several police officers ran out of the bushes toward her.

"The police raided the house and handcuffed everyone," she recalled.

Michelle also remembers sitting in handcuffs with her only concern being, "I am not going to get to use tonight."

She shook her head while talking to me saying, "I did not even care about my freedom. I went to jail charged with trafficking heroin, meth, and cocaine. They were even trying to charge me for organized crime."

She said it as if she was describing a life that someone else lived.

She went through a brutal detox in jail. She dealt with sweats, shakes, and horrible chills. A few days later, she was sitting in the laundry room in jail, waiting on laundry to dry. She had been put on laundry duty, and she was waiting to fold what was in the dryer when she saw a little Gideon Bible and read some of it.

"It planted a seed," Michelle said.

While she was in jail, her mom hired an attorney and called rehabilitation centers on her behalf. The judge allowed her to go directly from jail to rehab because, thanks to Carter, she had never been charged with a crime before this.

The bank foreclosed on her house. It was nearly empty anyhow. People who knew about the raid and had been to her house had stolen nearly everything in it, including a dishwasher, likely to buy and sell drugs.

She went to rehab thinking, "Something has to change for me. I have lost my daughter, my freedom, a marriage, my car, and my house." She was ready to stay in rehab and desperate for help and tools to stay sober. However, she learned soon after that insurance would not pay for rehab, so the center said she could not stay.

Michelle moved in with her stepdad and did ninety meetings in ninety days of both Alcoholics Anonymous and Narcotics Anonymous and even got a sponsor. Once again, she was committed to sobriety. She stayed sober those ninety days and started working at her family's company again.

Her life took a radical, positive turn. She was working the steps, doing online classes, and even got involved in a church. Ever since she had picked up the Bible in the laundry room, she had felt drawn to the idea of Christianity. She joined small group classes and went to every worship service the church offered.

Michelle also joined Noey's Mission, an outreach program at the church that gives away free clothes and food to people. Volunteers also pray and minister to people who want prayer and want to talk with people. Michelle explained that Noey's Mission felt that it was important that team members let people that came for clothes and food know they are loved, since many of them are struggling with addiction.

Michelle was able to reconnect with Carter too while he was going through his court dates and drug trial. Their relationship remained platonic, but they leaned on one another. As with Michelle, Carter had previously learned about God in prison.

"Carter had become really close to God and knew a lot about the Bible. He had binders and notes and his Bible was highlighted. He explained things to me when I had so many questions. He introduced me to Christian radio," she recalled. For a while both of them were sober.

But eventually, Carter relapsed. And after his drug trial, he had to go back to prison again.

Then Michelle relapsed, too.

But it would be the last time.

"At rock bottom, in the pit of despair, the most broken I have ever been, I returned to my mom's home and decided from that day forward that there had to be a better way to live," Michelle recalled. That day was September 22, 2015.

Tragically, almost a year later, Michelle found out over the phone that Carter died by suicide while in prison.

Reflecting on Carter's life and death, Michelle explained, "We tried for so long to save each other. I wondered why did I make it out and he didn't? Would it have helped if I had been there? I had talked him off the ledge so many times."

Michelle stood by Carter's grave and recommitted to God and to herself to stay sober. She vowed to Carter that she would never use again.

She has been sober ever since.

I asked Michelle what gives her hope. "God and recovery," she replied. I asked her what she meant by recovery. "Changing people, places, and things; developing a new circle of friends; and being welcomed with open arms at church," she responded.

What she had said was simple in that it was a mere sentence. But embedded in her words were life-saving decisions, actions, and mercy. Remaining sober meant healing from pain, a group of people to belong to, and a sense that her life had meaning and beauty. It meant security in her identity, leaning into God's grace and love. And it meant, in light of God's unconditional love, that in the place of shame there is dignity.

Kylen currently lives with Michelle full time, and Michelle is in charge of Noey's Mission now. Michelle lives the mantra, "You have to give it back to keep it," which refers to sobriety. She also regularly reminds herself, "progress not perfection."

Michelle is grateful that she has also become comfortable in her own skin. Currently, she is running her own legitimate jewelry business. Astonishingly, she has more than 165 women on her team.

"It is a close-knit circle of women. Same needs, but meeting them in new, healthy ways," she remarked. She explained to me that using drugs is rewarding so she realized she needed to replace those rewards.

When she tells me more about the group, the magnetism of her team makes sense. "We have a group chat. We cry and rejoice together. We uplift one another."

Reflecting on how far she's come, Michelle's face lights up with grateful joy as she says, "Now I am the leader of this incredible team. It is crazy how the tables have turned. Before I was taking, taking, taking, and now I am able to give good things to others. I am able to give and trust and love now openly because of how much grace and love has been given to me."

Michelle's story of her years of struggle with addiction and suicidal thinking is in many ways symbolic of the *true journey* to long-term recovery.

She has felt deep despair. She relapsed several times. She needed healing resources and other people's compassion and support.

Michelle's story is one of hope because Michelle has been able to make sense of where she has been and where she is going.

Michelle has a vision for her life, and crucially her vision is not simply about her.

On top of all of this, for Michelle recovery has meant recovering joy.

"I feel joy from connecting with God, using my story to help others and giving back to others," she explained.

It makes complete sense that Michelle is experiencing joy in her life because many things involved in Michelle's new lease on life cultivate joy.

Joy is often the result of discovering something (or someone) we love and giving ourselves over to it. Michelle is more familiar with joy these days because her life is lived for the sake of God and other people, for things beyond herself.

She is finding value and significance in her actions. Michelle feels as if her existence benefits and matters to others.

Michelle sees *the something more* in the activities and relationships that make up her life—motherhood, work, volunteering. She recognizes the truth, goodness, beauty, and meaning that are connected to those things.

This makes her life more fulfilling and thus more joyful.

Joy is what we feel when we imagine we are living for and living out a story that matters. The more we sense that this story is larger than ourselves, the more intense the joy.

9

Joy

Joy, on the other hand, seems to suggest a more ecstatic understanding of agency than "happiness" typically allows: an understanding of the human in which our action, our responsiveness, is solicited, to join in something larger than ourselves, as we are called into true communion with others, in richer, more exuberant life.

—Robert A. Emmons,
"Joy: An Introduction"

We had never been to Dany's house before, so we had no idea what sort of welcome we were in for. Dany's large table was covered with beautiful flowers and gold beads, reminiscent of the beads Dad wore in the Easter play so many years ago.

Her neighbors Jamie and Francis joined Paul, Dany, and me around the table for dinner. Dany brought out course after course until we were filled with calories and delight.

The large table was tucked in between two sides of Dany's massive, beloved and well-tended garden. Dany cares for it daily. Its lush, brilliant green leaves and bright pink and orange blooms felt like a warm embrace as we sat among them.

At the end of the meal, Jamie and Francis spontaneously asked whether we wanted to go jump into their pool and cool off. We changed into our swimsuits and began to walk down the long gravel driveway out to the street.

"This way," they said, pointing to a spot between the tall, gorgeous plants. We walked through the large plants and trees and discovered a silver ladder in the midst of the garden next to Dany's fence and just on the other side of the fence was another ladder.

Dany, Francis, and Jamie put ladders on each side of the fence so they could easily get to one another's houses. They could easily pop up and say hello, drop in on one another, and share space and conversation. Up and then down, we climbed from one side of the fence to the other.

If there is anything that I learned in the years following my family's weeks of hell, it is that we cannot make joy like we make spaghetti. It is not as if we can do this, then this, then mix that in, and—ta-da!—joy.

We cannot put joy on our to-do lists—it does not work that way—but we can put ladders up against fences. We can be ready and prepare. We can set another seat at the dinner table.

We can do things as part of our preparation that make it more likely that when joy is near we will be able to recognize it and embrace it.

And we can give ourselves over to the *what if?* of joy.

We all can live postured toward joy, *alive to its possibility,* even in the unlikeliest places, even in close proximity to our sorrow, even and most especially in the midst of our suffering.

Although joy is a gift, it has both a dynamic and *receptive* quality to it. So in addition to preparation, we can also look, listen, and be open to the awareness that any thing, any person, any idea could unexpectedly seize us with joy.

We often find what we are looking for.

It was not unusual for Steve-O's team and friends to receive an email describing a new idea for an extremely dangerous stunt; performing high-risk stunts was his job, after all. Steve-O is a stunt performer, actor, producer, and stand-up comedian who is best known for his role in the MTV series *Jackass*.

However, recipients were shocked by the tone and purpose of one particular email.

Steve-O had been evicted, and before leaving his apartment he wanted to ride a motorcycle out of his living room, jump onto the roof of the building next door, and then jump out of a window onto the sidewalk, landing in a hot tub. He said that if the team wouldn't help him set up the stunt he was going to do it anyway just to find out how many bones would be broken when he landed on concrete from twenty-five feet up in the air.

The email ended with, "I'm ready to die!"

Steve-O sent this email to nearly two hundred people. One of the recipients was his co-star and good friend, Johnny Knoxville. Johnny knew Steve-O was also abusing drugs and over time realized he was not just making jokes about edgy stunt ideas, but rather had become suicidal.

He took Steve-O's honesty seriously.

Johnny responded to Steve-O's honest cry for help by gathering a group of *ten of their closest friends* to show up to Steve-O's residence, stage an intervention, and take him to a psychiatric ward.

It is incredible to me to imagine a group of ten men walking together toward Steve-O's apartment. Steve-O's flourishing was a communal task.

His life was everyone's to keep.

Steve-O's honesty and Johnny's response to his honesty saved his life. After Steve-O got the help he needed, his joy was not his alone.

Thank God for friends like the pack of men who went to Steve-O's house.

Thank God for friends who take us and our honesty seriously.

A year and three months after my weeks of hell, Michaela, my treasured Los Angeles friend who is also an expert in making good decisions and throwing parties—an excellent combination—came to visit me in Connecticut.

I was still in my angry grief stage.

At that point, I had been in therapy for several months and I was still angry. Basically, everything about life continued to make me upset. She left her young child at home with her husband and took a red-eye flight to get to me.

She spent three days on my couch discussing my anger with me. I am not exaggerating. We hardly left the couch.

She told me she had never seen me so hurt, but she did not tell me to calm down. Michaela did not make me feel guilty or ashamed of the grief that was coming out in the form of fury. She did what I had needed for a long time.

She encouraged me to discuss my anger.

During Michaela's visit, I could not see any good or meaning—not in my weeks of hell, not in my work, not in where I was living, not in the future.

And she let that be okay. Michaela came to my place of anger and met me there.

Fear and anger obstruct joy—because even if we can still identify goodness, truth, meaning, or beauty, they seem too distant or disconnected from our reality—and they should.

Joy is "appropriately disturbed when the well-being of God's world is interrupted." The call to joy is not a call for everyone to be content with the status quo or to embrace any suffering that comes our way.

Fear and anger are fitting, meaningful emotions in our lives. Fear protects us sometimes, and anger can motivate us to change conditions that are oppressive or unfair.

On the other hand, fear can also paralyze us. Similarly, anger that is not worked through—confronted, discussed, acted out in constructive ways—can make us bitter and insufferable. And despair, as I have said, loves to feed on deep-seated, unprocessed anger and fear.

The ability to eventually welcome joy—to recognize and to realize relatedness—requires expressing fear and anger in productive, meaningful ways. In order for this to happen, "Feelings have to be mentionable," as Fred Rogers said.

The prison Bible study group was momentous in my life because it was a space where people could be vulnerable, weak, and broken.

We could feel any emotion and tell any type of story.

Similarly, Michaela's visit was pivotal because she helped me to work through my anger.

"All of us have invisible neon signs above us that signal to other people what we are willing to talk about, what is acceptable to share with us," what stories we are open to hearing, and what pain we are willing to witness.

More of us need invisible neon signs above our heads that indicate, "You can talk with me about anything. You can talk to me about your 'dark' emotions even. You can share what you are going through with me. I will even help you to *befriend* the emotions that you think are 'too bad' to share with anyone."

Befriending emotions starts with being able to discuss them. As therapists Alison Cook and Kimberly Miller describe, alongside others we can invite God to draw near to us in any difficult emotion and unburden us of the weariness we feel. We can allow God and our companions to help us to integrate the emotion into our lives in a helpful way.

Fear and anger can be fruitful.

Oddly, joy is another emotion that people often squelch. Joy is more likely to be a private matter. Like other powerful emotions, joy can be difficult for us, even terrifying, as researcher Brené Brown has discussed, because it requires vulnerability and courage. The moment we experience joy, we might wonder when we will lose it, or we might immediately anticipate that disappointment or disaster are sure to follow.

We also do not share our joy boldly lest we be seen as overly excited or too expressive. To display joy fully requires being "too demonstrative," "too passionate"—or so we might imagine. We may be anxious about being "too much."

Joy, like other emotions, longs to be shared though. Expressing joy, as with other challenging emotions, requires support.

Not only do we need permission to be honest about emotions like sadness, anger, and fear, we need permission to be joy-filled. And we need this permission from other people and ourselves. We can give one another and ourselves permission to experience joy in many ways.

One is to create spaces of joy.

Like preparing for joy (ladders against fences), we can organize spaces that are meant to invite and cultivate joy—spaces that suggest joy is both anticipated and welcomed.

When I was first invited to Shabbat at Yale's Center for Jewish Life by a student in Life Worth Living, I had no idea what to expect. I went because in my experience saying yes to invitations like this has affected my life in profound ways and helped me to better understand other people and cultures.

"Shabbat" refers to the Jewish practice of keeping Sabbath for twenty-five hours from just before sundown on Friday evening until nightfall on Saturday. It is one thing to read about Sabbath-keeping and another to witness it.

Much like at Dany's house, I was astonished by the welcome I received and by the joy I entered into. I was moved by the way the entire evening was set up for joy.

Shabbat at the center began with a worship service where the Sabbath was welcomed joyfully. There was dancing in circles along with special prayers, all energetically inviting Sabbath rest and celebration. People acknowledged the Sabbath like a friend and rejoiced that it had arrived.

It was fascinating to witness a group of people receiving a day of the week like this, greeting it as one would a beloved houseguest.

After the worship service, we gathered in a dining hall that had been specially prepared for hours before sundown so that no work would be done during the dinner. The tables were set, the candles were lit, and the food had been cooked.

Our only job was to eat course after course and talk about life as we enjoyed the meal and conversation with one another.

About an hour into the dinner, a man stood up on a chair and started clapping and singing loudly—no instruments, just his energy and voice and hands sounding together. He invited everyone in the room to join him.

We need other people to invite us to rejoice as much as we need other people to invite us to befriend anger and fear and openly lament.

We need to be trained in crisis care, and we need to witness pain and respond meaningfully to suffering—but we need joy too. At different points in our lives, our capacity for joy is enhanced or restricted by what we are facing. People have different capacities for joy.

Some people have a joyful disposition—what we might call the gift of joy—and simply find it easier to recognize and rejoice over the good, discover meaning, focus on beauty, and unearth truths that heal, so we desperately need each other.

The good news is that in the Bible "calls to rejoice are addressed to the *community as a whole*," as theologian Marianne Meye Thompson points out.

So it's all right that we need other people to help us recall, recognize, and reflect on the good. It makes sense that joy is a communal task the way the flourishing of Steve-O was a communal task.

We can rejoice together. If I am feeling as though I have no goodness to remember, no joy to recall, if my well is running dry, I can drink from your well of joy.

This is joy's gift. It is abundant. There is always more than enough. And it is even better when shared.

Before I knew it, we were all singing and clapping at the Shabbat dinner and even more people were standing on chairs and yelling out in high-spirited celebration.

Communal joy is mighty.

We did not hesitate. We could not help but join in. We smiled excitedly, and I'm pretty sure no one felt self-conscious about doing so. We joined and rejoiced and lived into the freeness of the space.

We gave ourselves over to joy.

"Joy is characterized by *freedom* manifested in play, in dance, in running, and leaping" and also "*vitality*, the feeling of aliveness," explains psychiatrist Warren Kinghorn.

Freedom needs room.

We clapped even harder and joined in singing the words, and the people sitting around me at the table looked at one another and laughed boisterously.

As I felt in this room and experienced in the prison Bible study, communal joy is a serious counteragent to despair.

"Joy is best experienced in community. Joy seeks company ('come and rejoice with me') and the company of those who rejoice feeds the joy of each," writes theologian Miroslav Volf.

Just as we need others to take our honesty seriously, we need other people to invite us out of the rut, to stand on chairs and clap, and to dance and sing.

Miriam the prophet famously took a tambourine in her hand and danced. Miriam and her people had been liberated, and she could not contain her joy. In an act of jubilation, she sang a freedom song and inspired others to follow.

Unfortunately, experiences of intense joy like the dancing and singing of Miriam and the one I was a part of at Shabbat are increasingly absent from American religious life. We tend to "convey the impression that joy should be the very last thing on our minds, or in our hearts, in our worship or in our relation to one another," writes theologian Rowan Williams.

If indeed joy is "the *tonality* of Christianity," as priest Alexander Schmemann contends, too many of us have forgotten.

It seems religious joy has somehow become less socially acceptable than celebrating a sports team victory. There are telling reasons people flock to stadiums and arenas. These are venues where feelings can be fully engaged because they are loud, huge places where numerous people are openly exhibiting their emotions. Plus, sports set aside places and times for letting go and giving ourselves over to something that feels meaningful to us, to something that is bigger than we are.

Interestingly, sorrow and joy are often intermingled in sports, as they were in Ezra's description of the temple being rebuilt. Sports fields and courts are places where we don't feel alone in our sorrow or our joy. Instead, during sports events, we recall what it is to feel truly connected to others, and thus more genuinely human, in the experience of what Brené Brown refers to as collective pain and collective joy.

Shared joy and pain are sacred experiences. "They are so deeply human that they cut through our differences and tap into our hardwired nature," Brown writes.

Human beings need physical and digital places where we feel we have the permission to openly lament—a gateway to joy—as well as places where we have the permission to openly rejoice over what is good, true, beautiful, and meaning-filled.

If we want more joy, we need more spaces like the Shabbat dinner I attended that actively invite it.

Joy

Trevor Henderson, Nashville's Opioid Response Coordinator, used to have a job in Hong Kong helping people to withdraw from heroin. This was before medication-assisted treatment. During their first forty-eight hours without the drug, he would sit with them and do whatever he could to soothe them, whether by making noodles at 2:00 a.m. or giving a shoulder massage as they cried.

Trevor knows how to be a loving witness who is truly with others in suffering.

Afterward, he helped people to get through their first thirty days of sobriety, too. One day, Trevor noticed kayaks near the treatment center, and he decided to rehabilitate them so he could take the guys out in the kayaks. He wanted to do an experiment, imagining that the rehabilitated kayaks might help the guys in their recovery.

There is something about seeing something repaired that gives us hope that we, too, can be mended.

Trevor also saw yachts near the shore and decided to seek out the yacht owners to ask for permission to let the guys paddle their kayaks out to them so they could jump off the yachts and dive into the water.

Several yacht owners gave him permission.

Trevor realized that inviting the men to move around outside seemed to be making a significant difference in their recovery.

It makes sense because spending time outdoors can actually help us think about the purpose of our lives. Being in creation can even renew our energy for living purposefully. Outdoor activities give us space to reflect as well as skills and attitudes that are required for feeling fulfilled.

In other words, human beings who are seeking healing need moments of recognizable self-transcendence. We need to see things that are beyond us, things that are bigger than our perspective. A mountain. An ocean. Water that rushes past the horizon. Buildings or trees you can't see the top of.

Trevor had another idea.

Trevor handed the guys snorkeling masks and buckets. He asked the guys to dive off the yachts into the water and collect mussels. The group of men kept doing this until buckets were filled with the mussels. Then they took the mussels back to the rehabilitation center and cooked and ate them together.

For many of them collecting mussels for food would have been a regular activity growing up. The collecting, cooking, and eating of mussels became a regular activity in rehab.

Over time Trevor recognized that these days together were contributing to healing joy in the men's lives. "There was always lots of laughter, and the guys began opening up as the days passed," Trevor reflected.

Suddenly, mundane practices like gathering food, cooking, and eating became fulfilling again for these men who had been escaping life rather than engaging it.

Those who opt for cheap distraction from the mundane and instant gratification over fulfillment and ultimate meaning will struggle to find joy.

Kayaking and mussel collecting helped the guys to experience a beautiful sense of belonging, a simple word to say, but also an extraordinary feeling that transforms. Belonging is not only a fierce motivator, but also a fierce counter to despair.

Many people struggle to feel like they belong because even when they are with other people, conversations are brief, hurried, shallow, and regularly interrupted. And too many of the activities we do together don't actually nurture meaningful connection.

We may find ourselves doing the same thing as other people around us, but it is not bringing us a deeper sense of relationship.

We share space—physical and digital—with each other, but we do not truly feel heard or seen.

If we want to heal despair, we have to regularly and meaningfully connect with others. We have to foster true belonging. And we need to heal our bodies.

We cannot simply think our way out of despair.

Trauma and pain reside in the body, not just the mind. So if we want healing from trauma, if we want to recover from pain, we need to be a part of communities like Trevor's in Hong Kong that cultivate belonging, while also regularly inviting us to enjoy tactile, life-giving activities.

Activities like cooking, crafting, building, hiking or walking, meditative breathing, playing a game, acting or role-playing, chanting, dancing, and making art are physical activities that promote wholeness.

There is a physical nature to joy.

Harmony, James, and I went to the prison to have a Christmas party.

We had so many women come to Bible study that we actually ran out of seats, so people had to sit on yoga mats. We realized on this night how lonely major holidays are in prison.

The prison did not allow the women to receive anything for Christmas from anyone or have any visitors on Christmas. Part of this is because some women would get gifts and visitors and others would not. However, the prison's method for preventing envy and pain also largely prevented joy.

It seems there must be a better way.

On this last gathering before the week of Christmas, our team wanted to encourage the women and provide gifts, so we got creative. We made two stacks of slips of paper. In one set, each piece of paper had a word on it and in the other set, each piece of paper had an encouraging Bible verse.

We explained the slips of paper to the women. Then, Harmony prayed over the words and James prayed over the pile of verses. In their own way, both Harmony and James asked God to allow the women to get the gifts that were meant for them.

Miraculously, a cardboard box happened to be in the room. I had never seen an empty box in the room before.

We filled up the cardboard box with the first heap of paper

slips. We passed the box around the circle and each woman picked out a word. The feeling of being given and getting a gift was more tangible than we had even imagined.

"This could be your word for 2019. This word can inspire, support, and embolden you," I explained.

We had seen the impact of words before.

Previously, we developed a reintegration ritual for the women. I tried to always have it with me just in case a woman told us she knew she was leaving prison before the next Wednesday night gathering.

If someone was about to leave prison, we would invite her to sit on a chair in the middle of the room and read these words over her:

> May Jesus grant you vision to see yourself as a new
> creation.
> May he give you strength to take up new habits.
> May he grant you mercy and surround you with people
> who believe in you.
> May he provide all that you need to flourish as a
> human being.
> May he help you to feel loved during both difficult and
> joyful moments.
>
> We pray we will see you again in this life, *but not
> in this room.*
>
> Isaiah 43:19–20 says:
> See, I am doing a new thing!
> Now it springs up; do you not perceive it?
> I am making a way in the wilderness
> and streams in the wasteland.

At the Christmas party, words were received and contemplated and rejoiced over by each of us in the room—words like possibilities, wisdom, trust, courage, power, restoration, resilient, capable, acceptance, enough.

Each word that was taken out of the box seemed to bring something to life in the receiver. We were reminded once again that words are powerful, that words create action, that words can nurture death and life.

Donna told us that they were two of the best presents she has ever gotten for Christmas.

The encouraging joy that these small slips of paper brought Donna was demonstrable. When we can look at something before us as Donna did—an object, something in nature, a moment, a person—and recognize, even if only for a few minutes, that there is something good, meaningful, beautiful, truthful before us and be grateful for it, joy is possible.

Joy often follows gratitude. Gratitude, like lament, can be a gateway to joy.

Dissatisfaction with what we have—whether it be our clothes, house, furniture, decorations, beauty products, body, devices, money, church, work, or relationships—makes it hard to be grateful.

Tomas Sedlacek writes, "What seems to compromise the feeling of joy the most is not evil per se, but the idea of *better*."

Of course, dissatisfaction, like anger, can lead to necessary change. But similarly to anger, fear, and pain, dissatisfaction (as well as scarcity and entitlement) hinders joy. So we have to determine how to make dissatisfaction, like pain, constructive.

And as best we can we have to figure out, as the women in the prison Bible study did, how to engage in beneficial dissatisfaction while continuing to look for opportunities to express gratefulness.

This means living in faith that even as we strive and struggle there will be moments in life when the grace of God is evident and moments for "gratitude for what life really is as the gift of God."

After each person in the room, including the team members, received a word, we put the slips of paper with Bible verses into the box and passed it around the room again.

Each person read the verse she picked out. It was remarkable to hear so many biblical promises and declarations read back to back. I don't think I had ever heard that many verses in a row from throughout Scripture.

Justina wept because she said she really needed to hear these words:

> "My grace is sufficient for you, for my power is made perfect in weakness." Therefore, I will boast all the more gladly about my weaknesses, so that Christ's power may rest on me. That is why, for Christ's sake, I delight in weaknesses, in insults, in hardships, in persecutions, in difficulties. For when I am weak, then I am strong.

Justina's weeping embodied why the prophet Jeremiah could say, "When your words came, I ate them; they were my joy and my heart's delight."

Near the beginning of Bible study that night, before anyone passed out or read anything, Ms. Aaliyah said she was scared about leaving prison in the coming months. So Harmony prayed right away for her.

Later in the evening, Ms. Aaliyah received these words from the box, "It is the Lord who goes before you. God will be with you; God will not leave you or forsake you. Do not fear or be dismayed." Ms. Aaliyah felt as if God had spoken right to her and had come to meet her right in the midst of her deepest need.

Rachel was already crying joyfully when we got to her turn to speak. Rachel had never come on a Wednesday night. She said that she prayed before bed a few weeks earlier that God would speak to her. After she prayed, she dreamed that night about the number 121. Rachel described waking up the next morning and reading Psalm 121, since Psalms is the only book in the Bible with over 120 chapters. Rachel said that the words from Psalm 121 had been comforting her for a few weeks.

And when she put her hand into the box, to her astonishment, she pulled out Psalm 121:1–2, "I lift up my eyes to the hills. From where does my help come? My help comes from the LORD, who made heaven and earth."

We were all filled with a stunned joy as Rachel explained her tears of delight after reading these verses. When we look for and notice that God is present to and active within our lives, it can bring us great joy.

While the women missed their families terribly, especially their children, and there were lots of sad tears too and sober conversation, for those two hours, joy was also felt. Like the land Ezra described where the temple was being rebuilt, there was room for our weeping and rejoicing to be held together.

Our brains are really good at remembering bad things that happen to us. In fact, one part of our brains in particular is "built to *look for* the bad." When something happens to us that is perceived as bad, our brain stores this memory carefully for future reference to protect us. This is obviously important for our well-being, but unfortunately it also means bad memories tend to trump good memories.

If we find ourselves consumed with bad memories, constantly focusing on what is horrible or lacking and on what meaning or truth has been lost, joy has a hard time making its way to us.

"We can close ourselves to joy. We can harden ourselves against it. We can be caught in the rut of life," Karl Barth explains.

The thing is, our brains are powerful. We can powerfully recall the bad, but we can powerfully recall the good too.

Astonishingly, I learned this from a six-year-old whose dad had just died. Her dad, Christopher, was my friend, and the day after his funeral I was sitting on the floor, playing with her, when Sophia suddenly brought up her dad.

"Do you think I could play chess like my dad did and win for him?" Sophia asked.

She was quite excited in this moment and spoke matter-of-factly. So I just looked at her with wet eyes and told her I thought this was a wonderful idea.

She went on.

I listened.

Sophia showed me photos of her dad that were on the kitchen table. She described each one carefully and exclaimed, "These photos are from my favorite trip with him! Will you come to my bedroom to look at one of my favorite photos?"

Of course I wanted to. I followed her into her bedroom, and she pointed to a photo on the mirror hanging on the back of her closet door.

She was standing in front of her dad. Her arms were open wide, stretched out to her sides at an angle. Her dad had his arms the same way, stretched out wide, but angled in a different direction. They formed an X with their arms.

I was so absorbed in the photo that I did not realize Sophia had gone to her closet to find the coat she was wearing in the photo. She put the coat on and stood in front of me, so she could see our reflections in the mirror.

She stretched out her arms the way they were in the photo.

"Will you put your arms out like my dad did?"

I looked in the mirror and extended my arms, trying to do exactly what Christopher had done in the photo.

With innocent jubilation, Sophia said, "We were just like this."

She smiled from ear to ear staring into the mirror.

It was as if the photo took her to another place, a world where the dad she loved so deeply was not gone, but intensely present. It is as if the joy she felt on that day, in that jacket, in front of her dad, standing in a silly photo, came over her once more; and perhaps even this time she felt that joy more acutely.

Such is the gift of retrospective joy, the joy that is found by calling to mind a moment when what you were doing, who you were with, what was happening was imbued with connection, with meaning.

I have recalled this moment many times over.

I could not have realized then how Sophia's wisdom would guide me, how the wisdom of a six-year-old would become essential for my understanding of joy.

No wonder Jesus said to let the children come to him.

Sophia's gift of backward-looking joy became a regular thing for me. It is a healing practice that I have done again and again. It is a way I feel joy, even and especially in sorrow.

Retrospective joy allows me to experience time with loved ones who once again come close to me and to others who love them so. Suddenly, they are not absent but mysteriously and powerfully near.

The fruit of backward-looking joy bursts through the pages of this book.

I told Paul in the summer of 2017 that I could not do Christmas as usual.

I could not imagine going to Kentucky and trying to celebrate Jesus's birth and open presents while reliving the week of Dustin's suicide and experiencing our family's first Christmas without Dustin, Mason, and Dad.

It was too much.

I insisted that we go somewhere warm, somewhere that was the opposite of every Christmas we had ever had. I needed to feel sunshine on my face.

I researched islands in the Caribbean and decided to learn more about Grenada because at the time there were relatively inexpensive flights there from New York.

I had hoped to actually go during Christmas, but it was far too expensive, so we planned to spend Christmas at home, just the two of us, and to find flights for the day before New Year's Eve instead.

I did not even know how to pronounce Grenada properly. I did not know where it was on a map. But I learned it was just north of Venezuela and so was quite warm. Compared to other places, it had inexpensive food and hotels and was incredibly beautiful, so I booked us tickets and found a little hotel across the road from the ocean for seventy-four bucks a night.

Chapter 9

Obviously, flying to an island to find some distance from grief is a privilege, and now more than ever I recognize how people who have the opportunity to decompress every once in a while by taking a vacation have a serious advantage when it comes to finding relief from life.

I realize how much the women in the prison Bible study could use a week like I had.

We woke up at 2:00 a.m. to fly to Grenada. After a bumpy two-hour bus ride with multiple stops from New Haven to the John F. Kennedy airport (if you've lived in the Northeast you know about these quirky long drives at odd hours that get you to your planes), we caught our flight to the little island of Grenada.

We settled into our little room after grabbing some dinner at a little food stand in the craft and spice market nearby. Miss Ruth cooked up fresh-caught fish with Cajun rice and plantains, which we would learn are standards in Grenada.

Miss Ruth can cook. Go see Miss Ruth if you ever find yourself in Grand Anse.

It was the night before New Year's Eve. After dinner we decided we needed to go to sleep, even though it was only 8:30. We were exhausted from less than four hours of sleep the night before and wanted to be able to stay up late for New Year's Eve. I leaned back into the bed, rolled around a bit to get the pillow right, and closed my eyes.

And then I heard the most awful sound.

I did not even talk to Paul about it; I just went down to the front desk to ask the hotel overseers about it. "Someone has an alarm going off in their room. Can you help?" I asked. One of the women walked up the stairs with me and paused to listen.

"That, do you hear that?" I asked.

She began to laugh. "Those are crickets," she said. "I'm not going to be able to turn down the crickets."

She promptly walked back down the stairs as I stood there in disbelief. "Oh my God," I thought. "My place for dealing with grief has a cricket problem? I need sleep so badly. This was supposed to be relaxing."

And then it hit me.

I mean like a freight train full of rainbows, the most warm, beautiful feeling overwhelmed my entire being.

Crickets remind me of being a small child. The cricket story was one of my dad's favorite stories to tell about me.

I was born with significant hearing loss, born legally deaf. My family did not know it until I was about one and a half years old. Over time, they recognized strange things that would happen during interactions with me.

For example, I was not an obstinate child, but they would call my name from another room and I would not come. This puzzled my parents. At one point I was playing on the floor with my back to my mother, and she called my name but I did not turn around. She got my dad, who then went to the kitchen and got two pan lids and banged them together a few feet from me, and I still did not turn around. They both realized then what Mom had known in her gut.

I could not hear.

My parents took me to different ear doctors until someone could help them figure out what was going on. Finally, a careful doctor discovered that I was born without middle ear bones.

In someone with usual hearing capacities, sounds pass from the eardrum to three small bones, known as ossicles. The bones of the middle ear transmit sounds into the inner ear, where they are converted into nerve impulses that are then sent to the brain.

Middle ear bones essentially tell your brain what you are hearing.

At that time in the early '80s, to my family's knowledge there was only one doctor in the United States who was doing the kind of surgery that I needed. He lived in Memphis, Tennessee, and even though there was no internet, my parents found him in their tenacious search for help. Another doctor in Winchester, Kentucky, knew about him.

My parents took me to this doctor in Memphis, and he told them about the surgery that he had designed. He explained that he was going to create prosthetic middle ear bones for me using my own skin and place them into my ears using a camera. It was an incredibly advanced surgery for the early '80s.

The doctor was uncertain of the results it would produce.

He told my parents that it might not work or that it could take months for me to be able to hear. And if I could hear, he could not guarantee what kind of hearing capabilities I would have. He was a Christian, so he and all of the nurses attending the surgery laid hands on me and prayed for me before beginning the procedure.

I faintly remember lying on the hospital bed in an oversized gown, being prayed over by a team of doctors and nurses.

After surgery I was in the hospital for a couple of days. Then my family packed up our red conversion van. Dad laid the seat flat in the back to make a bed for me. I slept most of the journey home. It was about nine hours.

Dad drove our van across the little creek in front of our house, the same creek Dad would later rescue Jenna's doll from. The hillside of trees across the road was dark since it was nighttime.

I was loopy from the medicine I was on. Mom helped me get out of the van. I was exhausted and drowsy. Suddenly, I covered my ears in pain.

Dad quickly came around the van and bent down toward me, worried. He wanted to know what was wrong. He always told me that in this moment, he was on his knee, looking into my face.

"The buzzing!" I had said. "What is the buzzing?" Apparently, I was still covering my ears. Puzzled, Dad listened attentively to the wondrous outdoors and he suddenly realized what it was.

"Crickets, Angela. Crickets are little bugs that live in the woods and near the creek. They make noise at night."

My parents wept big, warm, beautiful tears because they realized I had never heard crickets before.

As I was standing at the top of those stairs, there in that tiny Grenadian hotel, I felt Dad's presence in a way I had not since his death.

I felt his smile, his bright joy from that night so many years ago. I remembered how he would tell this story with such delight and describe the way he felt looking at me and realizing that crickets were just the beginning of the world that was about to be opened to me.

Joy

That night in my childhood driveway was indeed the beginning of lots of special moments in the weeks and months to come when I would hear all sorts of things for the first time—a dog barking down the street, a helicopter in the sky.

Adam Potkay brilliantly explains:

> Stories of joy begin in disunion, rupture, lack, and suffering. They climax, through some combination of striving, enduring, good luck or providence, in a (sometimes protracted) moment of (re-) union, plentitude, and harmony. Yet this resolution is not, or at least not fully, the result of individual agency. Rather, it is something in relation to which we are more or less passive, like infants or, in theistic models, children of God. The present or approaching good in which the mind most typically delights is a union or fulfillment that is not in our own power to effect. It comes to us, and it tends to come as a surprise.

On this night over thirty-two years later, listening to crickets in a country I had not yet learned to pronounce, what had felt broken was repaired. The man Dad was long ago, on his knee, rejoicing over the miracle that I could hear, was suddenly restored to me.

We were reunited, and for a short time I could recall clearly the man who lived and loved *BIG*.

It was a redemptive, restorative joy.

The next morning, Paul and I found a hotel about a mile from ours that was serving breakfast, and we ate and drank coffee outside under palm trees and singing birds for nearly three hours.

The manager of the restaurant said a band would be there that evening and we could come back and listen without needing a ticket.

Chapter 9

We were looking for easy New Year's Eve fun, and this was a perfect plan.

We came back to the hotel later that evening to find people crammed together under a tent listening to an incredible live band doing a mix of cover songs and originals. We had a rum punch and joined people on the dance floor.

Right before midnight, the hotel staff passed out champagne with nutmeg balls in each glass (Grenada is known for nutmeg). The band counted down, the clock struck twelve, and Paul and I kissed and sipped our champagne.

Then the band told everyone to head to the beach.

Shoulder to shoulder, a big group of us made our way through the sand, champagne glasses in hand, to watch fireworks. It was like a movie set. The sky was lit up on our right and on our left. Fireworks were being shot off of two piers over the ocean.

I became absorbed in the view. It was a new year. I had spent all of the previous year weighted down with grief, trudging through the silence, sorrow, fear, and anger. I took in a deep breath, the longest breath I had taken in a while.

Living in Los Angeles for thirteen years gave me an appreciation for ocean waves and taught me to listen to them and watch them closely. It was a huge reason I wanted to do this trip. Whenever I struggled to hear God's voice while living in LA, I would go to the beach, walk to the edge of the water, sit down, and be like: "God, I am looking for you. Of all places, I know you're here. We need to talk."

I imagine you have places like this in your life—places where you breathe deeply, places where you cry out to God, places that feel like home.

The beach is a home for me.

On the day we got engaged, Paul and I stood on the sand near the ocean and a pier in LA. Previously, we had officially become girlfriend and boyfriend while sitting in the sand near this same pier. During his proposal, Paul promised to me the promise of the ocean. For us, God's promise is evident in the ocean waves.

They always go out, but they always come back in.

Joy

It was there, on this New Year's Eve, standing in front of the ocean again with Paul, that I thought about this belief that has been so important to us. For over a year the waves had been going out and I felt like I was drowning. But on this night I actually could imagine the possibility of the waves coming back in.

Looking back, it seems the mere ability to imagine such a thing was the start to a year that would change my life.

I became open to the *what if?* of joy.

This imagining and the emancipating flood that was about to follow was made possible by the inbreaking of redemptive joy the night before.

Being in an incredibly different and new environment likely also helped me to see differently. It seems that no matter what means we have to make a shift in our environment—whether radical or small—simply changing settings is a helpful way to create space for change in our minds.

Paul and I decided to start the mile walk back to where we were staying and watch the New Year's Eve fireworks as we walked. We got about halfway when the skies abruptly opened and poured rain.

It was not sprinkling; this was a full-on Caribbean downpour. We began running immediately, but in less than a minute we were drenched.

The biblical image of water is restoration, renewal, hope. Jesus tells the unnamed woman at the well, whom I like to call Sarah, that he is in fact *living water*. Throughout the Bible water—like the ocean and downpour I experienced in Grenada—abounds.

My long dress was so soaked that I was having to hold my skirt in one hand so that I could run through the sand. But this rain was not like the rain on the night of Dustin's funeral in the park. And it felt entirely different from the rainy, dark evening in New Haven that followed the Package on the Porch Debacle just months earlier.

We began to laugh hysterically.

In between the bouts of laughter and the incredibly loud storm, I heard Paul yell out, "Change is coming!"

I knew immediately what he was talking about.

In films, whenever it rains it means that the story is about to change. The plot will take a massive turn. So whenever it rains in a film, Paul always says, "Change is coming!"

I immediately thought, "Yes, change *is* coming!" And I laughed even louder.

Moments later, I started crying. But not tears of sorrow as I had during the previous year. These were not muffin pan tears. These were tears of promise. These were tears of pure joy.

Indeed, sorrow is fertile ground for the blooms of other sorrows. But as Suzanne had promised, this ground is also somehow fertile ground for springs of new life to form within us.

Unexpectedly, it seemed as if a spring of new life was welling up within me.

What I did not know then was that the joy I felt as we ran in the rain was a futuristic joy.

Theologian Peter Leithart puts it this way: "Already we enjoy the fulfillment of what is not yet. And for this reason, thanks and joy invade our sorrows; the light of the coming day brightens the night. Deliverance is so utterly certain—it is in fact a *past* event, a *happened* not a *will happen*—that we can already give thanks for a rescue that is still future."

There is a joy that is "forward looking" too.

Perhaps futuristic joy is why on the cross Jesus could imagine *the joy set before him*.

It seems we can celebrate the goodness, the beauty, the truthfulness, the meaning that *will at some point come to be*—even while shrouded in sheer silence.

Futuristic joy comes from rejoicing that we will again glimpse meaning, beauty, truthfulness, or goodness and seemingly against all odds feel like we are connected to them, that they have something to do with our life.

The new life that was springing up in me while running in the rain, the forward-looking joy I experienced, was to come from unexpected places at unexpected times.

In the months that would follow, I was going to sit in a room with John and hear the word "relentless" and notice God's pres-

ence again. I was going to sit with college students in the Life
Worth Living class for a second semester and this time do what
I asked them to do—account for suffering in the good life.

I was going to rejoice unapologetically after realizing that
joy is neither naive nor frail, that sorrow wondrously can share
space with joy (as it already had in my life around the counter at
Stef's house).

Just a few months later, I was going to sit for the first time in
a circle on plastic chairs with women in a prison Bible study and
learn what it looked like and felt like to express joy as an act of
resistance against hopelessness.

Eventually, I was going to think back on the devastating week
of Dustin's death and realize that the moment in the park with
the star was indeed bright sorrow, God's withness and witness,
enigmatic joy in suffering.

Ultimately, this futuristic joy on New Year's Eve foreshadowed that I was going to discover, even when it seemed impossible, that during the grief that follows profound pain God can
mystifyingly give us a crown of beauty for ashes, joy instead of
mourning, and praise instead of despair.

When I first met Vanessa at the prison Bible study, I knew
I would love her. Her warmth and compassion can fill the emp-
tiest of rooms.

I loved the way Vanessa read the Bible, with conviction and
hope. She believed what she was reading, and you believed her
when she spoke into your life. She had a big presence and a grin
that suggested she was always critically thinking about how she
could respond next.

Vanessa had everyone's back.

Once, a woman who was newly incarcerated, Millie, came to
Bible study. She was scared of another woman on her tier who

had been bullying her. Vanessa told Millie what to do to resolve it in three steps, one of which involved writing a letter to someone with power at the prison. And when Vanessa realized Millie could not write, Vanessa took the pen and paper out of her hands and told her not to worry.

"I've got you," she said. "I'll write what she needs to know, and you can sign it."

The next week Millie came to Bible study happy to report that she had been moved to another part of the building.

Vanessa, like all of the women in the group, had her struggles, though.

She was in her early thirties and had wrestled with suicidal thinking since she was a teenager. She was in prison for hurting someone else when she had intended to hurt herself. And prison had not cured what she came to prison for.

One week, she was making plans and hugging everyone (against the rules), and the next she was telling me that making it through the day was tough.

On one particular Wednesday night, Vanessa explained to everyone that she was having to convince herself to live hour by hour. We did the only thing we knew to do: We prayed over her, begging God to let the darkness lift, and told her we loved her so. And we shared our stories, sang, and offered hope to one another.

As we all got up to leave, Vanessa came toward me and got close to my face, inches away, the way I had gotten close to Amy's when I told her I was so grateful she was alive.

"One more week," Vanessa whispered. "I will make it another week so I *will* see you next Wednesday, okay?"

My gaze locked with hers. I nodded my head yes and responded, "One more week."

The next Wednesday when Vanessa appeared and unceremoniously shuffled to her seat, my heart expanded.

After an hour of talking, the conversation turned toward the Bible text of the night, and Vanessa gasped. We were going to talk about the man at the healing pool and Vanessa was flabbergasted.

The morning after the last Bible study, the one where she said, "One more week," she found herself reading this story about the man next to the healing pool, whom Jesus told to pick up his mat and walk.

Vanessa had heard God saying to her, "Pick up your *burdens* and walk."

Vanessa's Bible guide had instructions to read part of First Corinthians that morning, but after mistakenly reading John 5 and hearing God say, "Pick up your burdens and walk," she was comforted and glad to be reading the "wrong" passage.

And here the story was *again.*

The God who sometimes is shrouded in sheer silence is apparently also the God of marching bands.

Indeed, Vanessa was walking forward with her burdens. She had made it another week, and while she had not found healing yet, she had kept her word.

Looking into one another's eyes was definitely a thing we did for each other in prison. Eye gazing was our superpower. And we were convinced that while prison could take away many things, it could not take away our words.

So we used our superpower and our words as often as we could.

One night we discussed truth-telling. Lots of people think truth-telling is what happens when we tell people what we *really* think in a counterfeit form of "love." On this Wednesday night, we talked about Christian ethicist Christine Pohl's version of truth-telling, the kind that affirms what is good and true in the world. If you do truth-telling right, if you learn how to recognize what is good and true and name it and celebrate it, truth-telling can lead to joy.

Joy is a celebration of the truth.

So we took the opportunity to apply Pohl's lesson. We decided to look at one another and tell the truth.

I stood in front of Rachel and read the words over her. Then Rachel read them over Jayla. Jayla read them over Miss Shirley, and then Miss Shirley read them over Amy, and Amy read them over Vanessa, and so on. Nia finished the circle by reading them over me. These were the words:

You are a child of God.
You are beautiful.
You are strong.
You are brave.
You are smart.
God has a purpose for your life.

We were trying to express that we belonged to one another and that our lives had value. During these minutes together we encouraged and affirmed the goodness within every person in the room.

It is important that we regularly take time to tell the truth to each other about our inherent value. We need to remind one another that we "don't have to do anything sensational to be loved."

In the midst of life's disappointments, mistakes, and failures, we especially need to stop and tell one another, "It is never too late. We are rooting for you."

We must not underestimate moments like this.

We still sat in a prison. These women still needed resources like holistic mental health care, sleep, mentorship, homes, and jobs.

But I saw the evidence in the room.

The empowered act of speaking the truth over someone else and having the truth spoken to us while tenderly looking at one another was transformative.

On my last night at the prison, Ms. Aaliyah said she wanted to sing me a song as a gift. She stood up confidently and began singing words from "Amazing Grace," loudly and off-key.

"Amazing grace, how sweet the sound that saved a wretch like me. I once was lost but now I'm found, was blind but now I see."

There was a long pause. She tried to go on but couldn't.

Suddenly, she shook her head, frustrated with herself, and sat down abruptly.

"I can't remember the rest of the words. I'm sorry."

I looked at her and said, "It's okay. Thank you, Ms. Aaliyah. Really. That was perfect."

My year at the prison had taught me that what she had done was more than enough. Her singing *was* a gift. Not because it was accurate in pitch and tone, but because it came from a place of confidence in the grace of God and was an act of faith and great love.

It was perfect because when I arrived at the prison one year earlier, I was lost. It was perfect because she and the other women had opened my eyes and helped me to remember what I had forgotten. It was perfect because she was singing truth over me. And I was rejoicing in it.

Before the women left the room that evening, I asked each of them for a big hug, the kind of hug I had been longing to give and receive for months.

It was fun to finally break this prison rule.

Right before switching off the lights for the last time, I looked around the room at the dingy carpet and the blue plastic chairs, and I thought about the condition of my soul.

The anger, fear, and profound grief I had first walked into the room with had over time been filled with mending joy.

I prayed that the women who could not be present that night, for whatever reason, could feel my love through the prison walls, just as we had prayed the night Amy was in mental health.

I walked down the sidewalk of that prison unbelievably grateful for everything the women had taught me, thankful for the way they had shared their lives with me and helped to renew my faith in the goodness of God. As I made my way to the front, I was amazed at the way regularly gathering with these women had changed my life.

They had given me the permission to be joyful while grieving, to dance and sing (off pitch) as acts of resistance to despair, to be honest, to mention every emotion. These women trained me to be prepared for joy anytime, anywhere, and not to squelch it, not to waver, but to give in to it.

They encouraged me to see the good, even as minuscule as it may seem, to find meaning in my family's suffering, to search hard for the truth and for beauty.

These women helped me to be thankful even as I was often dissatisfied and lamenting, and they gave me the sense of belonging that I had desperately needed for a year before arriving.

I walked out of all those locked prison doors imagining the day they too would walk out, hoping that somehow the healing and joy the women had brought me would be theirs too.

My colleagues at Yale asked me to give the last lecture of the semester for our Life Worth Living students. On Thursday afternoons, all of our sections gathered together in a large room to hear weekly lectures. I stood before the crowd of over one hundred people and sensed that the moment was significant.

For the seniors in the room, it was their final hour of class at Yale. For me, it was my last hour of teaching at Yale.

Of course, there was a lot I wanted to say. I wanted to make connections for them between what they had written in their final papers about what a life worth living is and what their next steps would be. I wanted to celebrate the meaningful conversations we had and the ways we had been changed by our time together.

But most of all, I wanted the last sentences of the lecture to convey what I had gained from the women in prison.

I gripped the podium and carefully scanned the room. I tried to look at the college students the way Amy, Vanessa, Miss Aaliyah and I had looked at one another during the significant moments we had shared.

And then I told the students some of the greatest truths I have learned.

Do not be afraid to tell someone that their life is worth living. Do not imagine that you have something more important to do than this. Do not imagine that there are more intellectual, deeper tasks.

Do it as much as possible.

Look people in the eyes and tell them that they matter, that their life *is* worth living.

I'm convinced that this simple but profound act can rescue others. It can even rescue us.

Epilogue

We can be united in our effort to heal opioid addiction and suicidal thinking as well as in our work toward a more just world.

If you are struggling with suicidal thinking, please call the National Suicide Hotline at 1-800-273-TALK (8255). Someone is there waiting to listen to you and to help you.

People are also currently working to establish 988 as the number for a national suicide prevention lifeline, just as 911 is the number for emergencies.

You can also google "suicide help" and you can chat with someone through the Suicide Prevention Lifeline website: https://suicidepreventionlifeline.org.

If you regularly think about dying by suicide, I hope you will develop a safety plan with a therapist. A helpful plan involves coping strategies for when you feel stressed, anxious, or depressed that do not involve self-harm as well as three people you can contact when you are experiencing suicidal thoughts. It can be as simple as having a plan to text one code word to a person you trust who will help you find healthy relief from your pain.

If you are struggling with opioid addiction and are ready to get help, you can call the Substance Abuse and Mental Health Services Administration's national helpline: 1-800-662-HELP (4357).

Whether you are dealing with addiction or thinking about suicide, there are things you can do to take steps toward finding healthy relief from pain:

- You can seek mental health care by calling a therapist in your area or contacting a person—such as a pastor at a local church, another type of religious leader, or a social worker—who can refer you to a therapist.

- If you are given medication for depression, anxiety, or some other form of mental distress, there is no shame in taking them and trying to find a cure through medicine.
- Aim to move your body twenty to thirty minutes a day. Take a walk or a hike. Ride a bike or go kayaking or swimming. Play a game. Try running or body weight exercises (there are tons of free resources online) or do yoga or take some other sort of exercise class (there are lots of free videos for yoga, and classes online too).
- Try to build and maintain relationships with others. There are support groups online, or you can use apps to find people in your community who like to do things you like. You can also find somewhere to volunteer your time, which can be a great way to meet other people and help you connect with things that are bigger than yourself.
- Try to find or create a group of people who listen to one another's stories, share joyful memories, and envision a future together.

Other activities that can be helpful include writing down or meditating on what you are grateful for, keeping a journal, writing stories or poetry, drawing or making other kinds of art (even if you don't think you are good at it!), coloring, gardening, playing music, sewing, cooking, or writing letters to friends and family.

Education and Prevention

Many people are working to reduce suicide and opioid addiction and overdoses, and they are doing incredibly meaningful things that you can be a part of.

The Madison Holleran Foundation (https://www.madison holleranfoundation.org) works to prevent suicides by assisting people during a crisis and also focuses on helping high school seniors and college freshmen transition to college. Carli Bushoven, the executive director of the Madison Holleran Foundation, talked about what this work means to her:

> Nothing you say or do can bring back a loved one lost by suicide. But that being said, showing up for these families, supporting them, showing them that mental illness and suicide isn't shameful, it can be talked about and the stigma can end. That is what has meant the most to me and my family. We have come a long way in recent years but there is still more work to be done. Seeing so many people, communities, schools, etc. trying to break the stigma and find resources and talk about mental illness just like physical illness is such a huge step in the right direction and it is so encouraging.

Suicide prevention and intervention by organizations like The Madison Holleran Foundation are essential.

Promoting suicide hotlines, sharing methods like ICARE that teach people to restructure negative thoughts, and knowing the steps to take if someone tells you that they are having suicidal thoughts are all critical for prevention of and intervention during suicide attempts.

David Laws is doing significant work on the front lines of the opioid crisis.

After Laura Hope died, David Laws helped found Georgia Overdose Prevention (https://www.georgiaoverdoseprevention.org) and committed himself to a life of advocacy and speaking. Wherever he goes he brings Laura Hope (in spirit and in a literal picture of her during her senior year) as well as his own recovery. The main mission of Georgia Overdose Prevention, where he is a board member, is to keep people alive until they get to recovery.

Together, David's and Laura Hope's stories have helped to pass vital laws that ensure people will not be prosecuted for dialing 911 and getting help when someone has overdosed, even if the callers have drugs present or have themselves been using.

He has also helped to promote other laws that have made Naloxone more widely available. Naloxone, if administered in time, reverses the effects of drugs like heroin, and kits that David has helped to pass out have saved over five hundred lives.

Importantly, David is also helping to lead the effort to help public policy officials and law enforcement to recognize that people struggling with addiction need access to adequate health care, not handcuffs.

Trevor Henderson, Nashville's Opioid Response Coordinator, is working with first responders. Trevor realizes that people who have overdosed are set up for success or failure based on how first responders do their jobs. It is essential that police, paramedics, and emergency room nurses treat people who have overdosed with compassion, rather than contributing to the shame those struggling with opioid addiction already feel. Trevor knows that first responders need to be equipped to connect people who have been rescued to resources that can get them into treatment.

Once a person has been saved after a near overdose or has decided that they are ready to receive help, medication-assisted treatment is the most effective way to get people on the road to recovery. Medication addresses the physical issues ("dopesickness") resulting from the brain changes that occur as a result of opioid use.

Medicine is another important element of care for people who are clinically depressed or have other psychological challenges related to suicidal thoughts.

Epilogue

Joining In

Better laws, better-trained first responders who keep people alive so they can get into treatment, handing out life-saving Naloxone, medication-assisted treatment, therapy, psychiatric drugs for mental illness, and education aimed at prevention—these are all *vital* in the effort to reduce opioid addiction and suicide.

Communities need more people helping in these efforts. We need a groundswell of people who care about preventing suicide and opioid overdose who will join people like Carli, David, and Trevor in their work.

There are a number of resources related to suicide help (websites, chat lines, and books) on this website: https://theswordmovie.com/resources/.

If you know someone who is currently struggling with suicidal thinking or opioid addiction and it is within your power to help them seek help, I encourage you to do so.

You can get guidance on suicide prevention by calling the National Suicide Hotline at 1-800-273-TALK (8255) or guidance on addiction by calling SAMHSA's national helpline: 1-800-662-HELP (4357).

You can take preventative measures in your home:

- Take every pill with "codone" in its name out of your cabinet and turn it in at a pharmacy that accepts drugs for safe disposal.
- Do not allow a doctor to prescribe opioids to anyone under eighteen.
- Do not have firearms in your home, especially if you live with people who struggle with depression, anxiety, loneliness, low self-worth, or meaninglessness. Over half of suicides involve firearms.

Warning signs of suicide include talking about suicide, about wanting to die, or about trying to find a way to die; reckless behavior; mood swings; increased use of alcohol or drugs; sleeping too little or too much; talking about life feeling meaningless; or demonstrating hopelessness, isolation, and withdrawal.

Warning signs of opioid addiction include drowsiness; slower thoughts; nodding off; loss of interest in grooming or personal appearance; reduced participation in activities that were once enjoyed; ignoring responsibilities; stealing from family, friends, or businesses; new financial difficulties; and isolation and withdrawal from family and friends.

If you feel powerless in your efforts to help someone you love struggling with suicidal thinking or opioid addiction or have lost someone to suicide or opioid addiction, I hope you will find a support group in your community or online where you can share your story and people can be witnesses to your pain.

If you want to help prevent opioid addiction and suicidal thinking, share warning signs online and with people in your circle of influence. Host conversations in your community about depression, anxiety, and despair, and nurture places where people can come together and share their stories and be encouraged to get the help they need. You can also donate to or volunteer for local or national organizations doing prevention and education work.

To understand more about why suicide happens, I encourage you to read Thomas Joiner's book *Why People Die by Suicide*.

To further understand the opioid crisis, I encourage you to read Beth Macy's book *Dopesick* and Andrew Sullivan's article in *New York Magazine*, "The Poison We Pick."

Fentanyl and Disparities in the Opioid Crisis Narrative

Opioid addiction and opioid overdose death rates are soaring in all types of communities and among people of all different statuses and ethnicities. Overdose rates are dramatically rising because people, often unknowingly, are taking substances laced with fentanyl—like heroin, counterfeit pills (e.g., oxycodone or Xanax), meth, and cocaine.

According to Trevor Henderson, Nashville's opioid response coordinator, and other people on the front lines of the opioid crisis, fentanyl has become our primary problem. Reporter David Armstrong powerfully warned in 2016 that "fentanyl is poised to become the *catastrophic exclamation point* to 20 years of escalating opioid addiction in the United States."

While white Americans use opioids at higher rates, the rate of deaths related to opioids has been increasing more quickly among Americans who are Black or of Latin American descent due to a combination of fentanyl-laced substances, lack of access to treatment, and exclusion from the opioid narrative.

The beginnings of the opioid crisis have most commonly been traced back to over-prescription of incredibly addictive pain pills in white rural communities during the 1990s. However, heroin has been destructive to the lives (and therefore the families) of Black Americans in urban communities since the 1970s.

In both rural and urban communities, opioid use has been coupled with economic devastation.

In the early 2000s opioid addiction spread from predominantly white rural areas to white suburban communities and middle-class families and thus caught more mainstream attention.

Mass Incarceration and the Prison Reform Movement

Alongside education and prevention related to suicide and the opioid crisis, it is important to understand the history of the prison system in the United States, what is known as "mass incarceration," and the work people are doing to reform or even abolish our present prison system and what they have in mind that we should do instead.

Alarmingly, Americans have learned very little from the response to the surge in crack cocaine use in the 1980s and '90s.

The response to crack cocaine (as opposed to cocaine, which is more expensive, has historically been used by wealthy, mostly white people, and has had less harsh punishments) was mass incarceration.

Similarly, heroin addiction among poor people has led to further mass incarceration.

Here's the thing: years of drug-related mass incarceration have done little to curb the cocaine issue in America. Cocaine is still a major problem. Among illicit drugs, cocaine is the second most frequent killer.

So now both crack and heroin addiction are major crises in the United States because, instead of attempting to understand and heal root causes of addiction, we view addiction (as I did with Dad) as a moral failure.

Not only are we spending massive amounts of money and imprisoning countless people who are addicted to substances rather than helping them to get true healing, but there are economic and racial disparities at every level of the criminal justice system.

Boys who grow up in the bottom 10 percent of income for families—families making below $20,000 a year—are *twenty times* more likely to end up in prison than boys who grow up in families that make more than $143,000 a year. And while Black and white Americans use drugs at *similar rates*, Black people are imprisoned for drug charges at a rate nearly *six times* that of white people.

Online, the Sentencing Project has a graph of human figures representing people born in 2001. Some figures are gray, and others are orange. The people in orange will likely go to prison one day. Looking at the chart is a punch in the gut. Based on current trends, one in 111 white women, one in forty-five Latina women, and *one in eighteen* Black women born in 2001 will likely go to prison.

The chart is even more staggering for men. One in seventeen white men, one in six Latino men, and *one in three* Black men born in 2001 will end up in prison at some point in their lifetime.

To learn more, please watch the films *Just Mercy*, *13th*, and *When They See Us*. Please also read the books *Just Mercy* by Brian Stevenson, *The New Jim Crow* by Michelle Alexander, *American Prison* by Shane Bauer, and *Stamped from the Beginning* and *How to Be an Antiracist*, both by Ibram X. Kendi.

If you are able, volunteer at a prison or become pen pals with someone in prison.

Epilogue

To read about prison reform specifically, visit the Equal Justice Initiative's website (https://eji.org/criminal-justice-reform/) and the Charles Koch Institute's website (https://www.charleskoch institute.org/issue-areas/criminal-justice-policing-reform/why -prison-reform-matters/). There are also groups working to abolish the current prison system in the United States. You can learn more at Critical Resistance and The Marshall Project websites and by reading Gabriella Paiella's article on transformharm.org, "How Would Prison Abolition Actually Work?"

—————

I hope you will be part of a groundswell of people who come together to discuss the roots of despair and scrutinize our contemporary visions of what a good life is. I hope you will join in the important work of reducing suicide, healing addiction, and changing the prison system. I hope you will create and nurture a community that focuses on understanding, recalling, and being open to joy.

Gratitudes

This is my love letter to the people who bring my life unspeakable joy and have made this book possible.

Family

Paul, you have kept your vows to be faithful on every kind of day. You endured the worst weeks of life with me, and we walked together through the darkest years afterward. Thank you for helping me get to the hospital to see Dad before he died and for all you did with our family the week that Dustin died. Your presence, gentleness, compassion, and strength were so needed. On the most difficult days you stayed near. I love you. Thank you for reading this book ahead of time and for listening on so many days as I verbally processed how emotionally difficult it was to write.

Jenna, my dear little sister. I could not have held Dad's right hand without you holding his left hand. We have stood on such holy ground together. Thank you for everything you did to try and help Dad and for all you did for our family during those tragic weeks. I am so grateful for your close reading of this book and for your willingness to let me tell *our story*—and especially for your willingness to let me use some of your words to tell it. We shared a bedroom as kids and live near each other today, and you remain one of my closest companions. I am so thankful we could fly together to be with Stefanie and Allison in Albuquerque for Mason's funeral.

To you and my other wonderful sisters, Stefanie and Allison, and to my amazing niece Natalie, those hours mourning Mason around that kitchen counter are among some of the most sacred of my life. Stef and Alli, I also want to thank you for reading this book for accuracy and for being open to allowing me to share such intimate parts of our lives. I love you so much.

Rob, you were a witness to everything. You also rushed to the hospital. You went everywhere we needed to go on the day Dad died. Thank you for all that you did and do now to love my sister and our family well. I am so glad you are my brother-in-law.

Mom and Don, you were with us during those distressing weeks—also crying, looking on, being with us, suffering with us, helping in every way you could, even as Don was having heart surgery. Don, thank you for coming to Dad's funeral the day after you had surgery. It meant the world to me. Mom, thank you for every card and phone call in the years that followed, for every visit, for every moment that you prayed my grief would lift. I love you both tremendously. Thank you for reading this book and being wonderful parents who care so deeply and celebrate so loudly, and who are willing to always listen and come when you are needed.

Shannon, you made sure Dustin's funeral was a true celebration of who he was, and it was incredibly meaningful. To Dustin's parents, I so appreciate your emails. From the bottom of my heart, thank you. To Dustin's siblings, you honored your brother with love that to this day moves me.

To the many other family members and friends who attended Dustin's, Mason's, and Dad's funerals, thank you. Looking out and seeing you there was so significant. I am so grateful for those of you who have listened, prayed, texted, and sent cards.

Michelle, my dear sister-in-law, I had no idea how much our Skype conversation would affect my life. Thank you for sharing your suffering and subsequent recovery journey with me and allowing me to write about it. Your encouragement has meant so much. May sobriety and joy always be yours.

Friends

Sarah and Ronnie Farmer, thank you especially for the meal and conversation following those horrifying weeks. Paul and I are grateful for your enduring friendship and prayers (and our dance parties with your beautiful children!). We love you.

Molly Galbraith, after nearly twenty-five years of friendship, my heart continues to overflow with gratitude for you. Your gifts are constant reminders of your care and thoughtfulness. You are so loyal, so kind, so hardworking, so courageous. You embody the poise and strength of your mother (the pitbull in pink!) and the imagination and inspiration of your father.

Macy Workman, since college our talks have filled up my soul. I always marvel at your grace, mercy, and ever-expanding resilience. You are always, always there for me. You are postured for joy like no one else I have known.

Beth Chiaravalle McQuitty, your table is long; it always has an extra seat for anyone who needs one. You love so deeply, and you are always willing to drop everything and be an incredible friend. Thank you for the way you listen, for your beautiful, compassionate heart, and for the enthusiasm you bring into every room you enter.

Michaela O'Donnell Long, your wisdom is incredibly important in my life. Your ability to stimulate new dreams in me every time we text or chat never ceases to amaze me. I can't wait until we create something together. Thank you for reading this book as I wrote it and supporting me every step of the way. You are brilliant and fierce and caring.

Liz McQuitty, your preaching, like your conversations with your friends, is always perceptive and thought-provoking. Your visit to Waco (coming to my class!) is a beautiful symbol of the kind of friend you are to me. I am grateful for your support, care, and encouragement.

Lyndsey Deane Ratchford, your passion and energy are contagious. You love and think big. I appreciate the way you can always envision a better future, the way you embody hope. Thank you for championing other people's lives—like mine—as if they were your own.

Chloe James, our phone chats and my LA visits—when I slept on your couch and we swam in the ocean and stayed up way too late—sustained me during the most difficult years of my life. You continuously believe in me. Thank you for always looking me in the eyes and emboldening me and telling me what you see in me. It has made such a difference.

Katie Eischen, our years of friendship and recent conversations have been such a source of love, truth, and goodness in my life. Thank you for your prayers, for contributing to Dad's funeral costs, and for visiting us. You are always so good to me.

Molly Stuckey, thank you for endlessly cheering me on. Truly, we grew up together and found ourselves alongside each other. Your enthusiasm and passion for life's biggest and smallest joys are infectious.

Mary Alice Birdwhistell, thanks for the four-hour dinner that immediately made me realize I could trust you as a friend and as a pastor. Your sermons and our talks about life and death and everything in between are a gift.

To the remarkable women of the TBB (and their awesome families)—Anne Jeffrey, Devan Stahl, Katie Larson, and Sarah Mosher—our regular gatherings and your willingness to listen, talk, celebrate, and pray have made life in Waco exceptionally meaningful and joyful. My heart overflows with gratefulness for our instant and ever-blooming friendship.

People who made this book possible

To the other beautiful souls who shared their stories and thoughts with me for this book—Lynn Harper, David Laws, Carli Bush-oven, Trevor Henderson, and Nina Lau-Branson—it is difficult to express in words how deep my gratitude is for you.

To the prison Bible study team, you taught me so much. What an honor to serve alongside of you. Our car-ride conversations and singing together in that prison room are imprinted on my heart forever.

To each person I met while writing this book who has known someone who died by suicide or opioid use and shared their story with me and encouraged me, I see you too. I am grateful for your vulnerability and care.

Gratitudes

To each person I met while writing this book who has struggled with suicidal thinking and addiction, you are not alone. I see you. May you have enough mercy to carry on and enough compassion to pursue sobriety.

Ryan Ramsay, your amazing editing skills and careful attention to the mundane but incredibly important details of this book were essential. Thank you for your friendship too.

Joy Moton, your passion for interviewing, storytelling, and writing in the name of Jesus and in reflection of God's love is inspiring. Thanks for your partnership in this endeavor. I look forward to reading more of what you write in the coming years.

Sarah Schnitker, thank you for reading this book in its initial stages and for your friendship. Your enthusiasm is contagious and your "we can do this" attitude and willingness to always partner is so needed (in higher education) and beautiful.

Sara Barton, thank you for your encouragement as I was writing this book and for our meaningful conversation that reminded me that I am not alone.

To Dean Todd Still and Associate Dean Dennis Tucker, thank you so much for your support and for creating space in my first year at Baylor to write and edit this manuscript. To my colleagues at Truett, thank you for your encouragement and prayers.

Ryan McAnnally-Linz and Matt Croasmun, each step of the way you have believed in this book. Thank you for introducing me to David Bratt, for reading chapters, for giving me opportunities to share from the book in front of audiences, for celebrating it, and for praying for me and my work. I am especially grateful for what you said on our hike in Texas. Your friendship and collegiality mean so much to me. Cheers to Lausanne and our other wondrous adventures in the past (as well as those yet to come).

To all of my colleagues at the Yale Center for Faith & Culture, I am so grateful for you and the years we spent investigating joy together. Thank you for our morning prayer times, for crying with me in those dark hours, for listening when I know you had so much to do, for being witnesses to my pain.

Special thanks to Miroslav Volf and Phil Love for your leadership of the Joy Project, your incredible wisdom, and your commitment to the life and teachings of Jesus.

To each person at Eerdmans who helped to get this book ready for publication, thank you. I am especially grateful to Jenny Hoffman and to copyeditor Jeff Gifford for your careful attention to the details of this manuscript.

David Bratt, my amazing editor and friend: we sat down at a white, boring table in a loud, ordinary room in November 2018 and had one of the most arresting, uplifting, extraordinary conversations of my life. I told you about this book and you read some of its pages, and you instantly believed it could make a difference. I was inspired and moved by your care for my story and my passion to address suicide and opioid addiction. You have championed this book every step of the way. Your ideas and editing have elevated my work. I cannot thank you enough.

Laura Bardolph Hubers, director of marketing and publicity extraordinaire, thank you for reading this book so carefully and lovingly. Thank you for your investment in its purpose and for every ounce of energy you have poured into inviting people to read it.

David and Laura, thank you for who you are as human beings and for choosing to do ministry by partnering in the creation of books—for still believing books can change things.

Notes

A Note about How This Book Came to Be

xii *This book shares* The opinions expressed in this publication are mine and do not necessarily reflect the views of JTF or the people who participated in the Joy and the Good Life project. For more information on the project, see the Yale Center for Faith and Culture's website (http://faith.yale.edu).

Chapter One

3 *"Anthony Bourdain devoured the world"* Frank Bruni, "The Insatiable and Unknowable Anthony Bourdain," *New York Times*, June 8, 2018, https://www.nytimes.com/2018/06/08/opinion /anthony-bourdain-suicide.html.

3 *Anthony Bourdain spent decades* Brian Stelter, "CNN's Anthony Bourdain dead at 61," *CNN*, June 8, 2018, https://www .cnn.com/2018/06/08/us/anthony-bourdain-obit/index.html.

3 *"Bourdain's image"* Bruni, "Insatiable and Unknowable Anthony Bourdain."

4 *"In his writing"* Bruni, "Insatiable and Unknowable Anthony Bourdain."

9 *"To be an educator"* Thomas Groome, *Educating for Life: A Spiritual Vision for Every Teacher and Parent* (New York: Crossroad, 1998), 35.

12 *"In this course"* Matt Croasmun, the Life Worth Living Director at Yale College, helped me to shape the words in this paragraph in the introduction to the course. Some sections are

exactly his words from the introduction he gives on the first day of his course.

17   *Our dad lived BIG*   I am grateful to my sister Jenna for allowing me to use words she shared in her eulogy at our dad's funeral in my descriptions of Dad throughout this book. Special thanks for this section on how Dad lived big: Jennifer Olney, eulogy for David Lee Williams, January 24, 2017.

Chapter Two

23   *His heroin dealer*   David Armstrong, "Dope Sick," *Stat News*, August 2, 2016, https://www.statnews.com/feature/opioid -crisis/dope-sick/.

23   *DJ was dead*   The US Centers for Disease Control and Prevention reports that approximately 115 people die every day in the US from opioid overdose. Centers for Disease Control and Prevention, "Understanding the Epidemic," https://www.cdc .gov/drugoverdose/epidemic/index.html.

23   *On April 21, 2016*   Enjoli Francis, "Police Release Findings into Prince's Death, Giving Glimpse into His Final Days," *ABC News*, April 20, 2018, https://abcnews.go.com/US/police-release -findings-princes-death-giving-glimpse-final/story?id=54619 334.

24   *At just five feet two*   Kory Grow, "Prince Dead at 57," *Rolling Stone*, April 21, 2017, https://www.rollingstone.com/music /music-news/prince-dead-at-57-62331/.

25   *The move in*   Beth Macy, *Dopesick: Dealers, Doctors, and the Drug Company That Addicted America* (New York: Little, Brown, 2018), 123–26; see also Andrew Sullivan, "The Poison We Pick," *New York Magazine*, February 19, 2019, http://nymag .com/intelligencer/2018/02/americas-opioid-epidemic.html.

29   *If so, since you began*   At the time of this publication, someone was dying of opioid overdose every eleven minutes. See "Every 11 minutes someone in America dies from an opioid overdose," The Truth website, https://opioids.thetruth.com/o/the-facts /fact-1005. Website factoid drawn from Holly Hedegaard, Arialdi M. Miniño, and Margaret Warner, "Drug overdose deaths

in the United States, 1999–2017," NCHS Data Brief, no. 329 (Hyattsville, MD: National Center for Health Statistics, 2018), https://www.cdc.gov/nchs/products/databriefs/db329.htm.

29   *For one thing*   Sullivan, "The Poison We Pick."

Chapter Three

51   *"Grief is a lonely"*   Glennon Doyle Melton, Instagram post, December 23, 2018.

Chapter Four

61   *People have shared reasons*   While all the recent major commentaries I consulted contain helpful notes on this text, I found George R. Beasley-Murray's helpful in providing a brief, approachable account of major interpretive options: George R. Beasley-Murray, *John*, Word Biblical Commentary (Nashville: Thomas Nelson, 1999), 188. Interested readers should also attend to Charles H. Giblin, "Suggestion, Negative Response, and Positive Action in St John's Portrayal of Jesus," *New Testament Studies* 26, no. 2 (January 1980): 197–211, esp. 208–10. Several recent commentators have relied on his argument for their interpretations of the passage.

61   *"I have said that"*   Wilde, *De Profundis*, 71.

62   *"Where you take"*   Seneca the Younger, *On Anger* 2.31, as quoted in Martha Nussbaum, *The Therapy of Desire: Theory and Practice in Hellenistic Ethics* (Princeton: Princeton University Press, 2009), 388. The quotation, curiously missing a reference, seems to be Nussbaum's translation of *ubi maxime gaudebis, maxime metues*. See Seneca, *Moral Essays*, vol. 1, trans. John W. Basore, Loeb Classical Library (Cambridge: Harvard University Press, 1928), 388. For an updated translation (with an updated title), see Seneca, *How to Keep Your Cool: An Ancient Guide to Anger Management*, trans. James Romm (Princeton: Princeton University Press, 2019). For help in tracking down this rather difficult quotation, I thank Ryan Ramsay, Ryan McAnnally-Linz, and Karin Fransen.

64   *"You will cease"*   Seneca, *Letters from a Stoic* 4.3, trans. Robin Campbell (New York: Penguin, 1969), 38. Seneca is actually quoting Hecato, another Stoic philosopher, whose work is unfortunately lost.

64   *"The anticipation of joy"*   Jürgen Moltmann, "Finding Joy with Jürgen Moltmann," video on Yale Center for Faith and Culture website, September 24, 2014, https://faith.yale.edu/news/finding-joy-jurgen-moltmann.

67   *"In the Western world"*   Soraya Chemaly, "Why Women Don't Get to Be Angry," *Medium*, September 18, 2018, https://medium.com/s/story/rage-becomes-her-why-women-dont-get-to-be-angry-b2496e9d679d.

67   *Angry women are often categorized*   J. M. Salerno and L. C. Peter-Hagene, "One Angry Woman: Anger Expression Increases Influence for Men, but Decreases Influence for Women, During Group Deliberation," *Law and Human Behavior* 39, no. 6 (December 2015): 581–92.

69   *I definitely did not*   Kate Bowler, *Everything Happens for a Reason: And Other Lies I've Loved* (New York: Random House, 2018), xvi, 170.

Chapter Five

78   *Most of the women*   Stephanie S. Covington and Barbara E. Bloom, "Gendered Justice: Women in the Criminal Justice System," in *Gendered Justice: Addressing Female Offenders*, ed. Barbara E. Bloom (Durham, NC: Carolina Academic Press, 2003), 12.

79   *In prison, you are your sins*   Jürgen Moltmann highlights this predilection toward seeing a human *as* her action as contrary to the freedom of the gospel. Continuing to see a person as her deeds—whether good or bad—*dehumanizes* and robs a person of their *given* worth by virtue of being freely created by God. Moltmann demonstrates that seeing a person as virtuous is simply the flip side of seeing them as a sinner. For either kind of seeing to take place, one must first and foremost view a person

as their deeds rather than as freely created and freely given grace. Jürgen Moltmann, *Theology and Joy*, trans. Reinhard Ulrich (London: SCM Press, 1973), 65–67.

81 *"Today, there are more people"* The Sentencing Project, "Criminal Justice Facts," The Sentencing Project website, https://www.sentencingproject.org/criminal-justice-facts/. Emphasis added.

81 *Approximately half of the people* The Center for Prisoner Health and Human Rights, "Incarceration, Substance Abuse, and Addiction," web page, https://www.prisonerhealth.org/educational-resources/factsheets-2/incarceration-substance-abuse-and-addiction/; Friends Committee on National Legislation, "Sentencing: A Major Driver of Mass Incarceration," web page, https://www.fcnl.org/updates/sentencing-a-major-driver-of-mass-incarceration-184.

82 *Many of the women* Carissa R. Violante, "Opioid Crisis Roadmap Overlooks Gender," Women's Health Research at Yale website, January 7, 2019, https://medicine.yale.edu/whr/news/article.aspx?id=19129.

82 *In fact, 80 percent* Wendy Sawyer and Wanda Bertram, "Jail Will Separate 2.3 Million Mothers from Their Children This Year," Prison Policy Initiative website, May 13, 2018, https://www.prisonpolicy.org/blog/2018/05/13/mothers-day-2018/; Dorothy J. Henderson, "Drug Abuse and Incarcerated Women," *Journal of Substance Abuse Treatment* 15, no. 6 (November–December 1998): 579–87.

82 *One study I found determined* James M. Conway and Edward T. Jones, "Seven Out of Ten? Not Even Close. A Review of Research on the Likelihood of Children with Incarcerated Parents Becoming Justice Involved," Central Connecticut State University, 2015. Claims about the likelihood vary widely—some with better evidence than others. See also Prison Fellowship, "FAQs about Children of Prisoners," web page, https://www.prisonfellowship.org/resources/training-resources/family/ministry-basics/faqs-about-children-of-prisoners/#Child_going_to_prison.

84 *Dealing with past trauma* Joanna Moorhead, "How Dealing with Past Trauma May Be the Key to Overcoming Addiction," *The Guardian*, November 24, 2018, https://www.theguardian

.com/lifeandstyle/2018/nov/24/joanna-moorhead-gabriel-mate
-trauma-addiction-treat?fbclid=IwAR1f2L_h6sKC4_OY-G-i
-K5_UAiRqgAyM1VQnurcJGWxoh6ecwaFJDIUr6k.

86   *We were in the middle*   Matthew Croasmun, *Let Me Ask You a Question: Conversations with Jesus* (Nashville: Upper Room Books, 2018).

89   *Joy gathers*   Willie James Jennings, "Joy That Gathers," consultation on "Religions of Joy," Yale Center for Faith and Culture, New Haven, CT, August 21–22, 2014. For the basic ideas he gives in this paper and the lecture he subsequently gave at the Joy and the Good Life conference, see the brief video, "Willie James Jennings on Joy That Joins," https://www.youtube.com/watch?v=CwiFx_mJAl4.

89   *Our music became*   Willie James Jennings, Joy and the Good Life conference, Yale Divinity School, New Haven, CT, July 2018, and Almeda Wright and Anne Wimberly, "Memory and Joy," Lecture for the Youth Ministry Institute, Yale Center for Faith and Culture, May 3, 2017. For the basic ideas they give in this lecture, see the brief video: "Dr. Almeda Wright & Dr. Anne E. Streaty Wimberly—Memory & Joy," Yale Youth Ministry Institute, June 13, 2017, https://www.youtube.com/watch?v=8hOO96TzVR4.

90   *Suddenly, we were rejoicing*   Marianne Meye Thompson describes this as *joy notwithstanding*, joy that looks "forward in hope anticipating the action of God to remove all affliction and tribulation," in her chapter "Reflections on Joy in the Bible," in *Joy and Human Flourishing: Essays on Theology, Culture, and the Good Life*, ed. Miroslav Volf and Justin Crisp (Minneapolis: Fortress, 2015), 20, 25, 33.

90   *"You're not defenseless"*   This line is in Lauren Daigle's song, "Rescue," from her album *Look Up Child* (Franklin, TN: Centricity Music, 2018).

93   *"What is the difference"*   Christian Wiman, *My Bright Abyss: Meditation of a Modern Believer* (New York: Farrar, Straus and Giroux, 2013), 53.

95   *"The word for joy (chara)"*   Jürgen Moltmann, "Christianity: A Religion of Joy," in Volf and Crisp, *Joy and Human Flourishing*, 12.

95   *Joy has a "too-muchness"*   Charles Mathewes, "Toward a Theology of Joy," in Volf and Crisp, *Joy and Human Flourishing.*

96   *Joy is an experience*   Caroline Ainsworth was a member of the
Joy and Adolescent Faith and Flourishing Committee. Caroline
described joy this way during a meeting for the Joy and the
Good Life Project.

96   *It was in this prison*   Jennings, "Joy That Gathers."

96   *Against all logic*   Jennings, "Joy That Gathers."

Chapter Six

99   *For every suicide*   American Foundation for Suicide Prevention, "Suicide Statistics," web page, https://afsp.org/about-sui
cide/suicide-statistics/.

99   *Suicidal thinking is highest*   Centers for Disease Control and
Prevention, "Suicide: Facts at a Glance 2015," web page, https://
www.cdc.gov/violenceprevention/pdf/suicide-datasheet-a.pdf.

99   *While young people report*   National Institute of Mental
Health, "Suicide," web page, https://www.nimh.nih.gov/health
/statistics/suicide.shtml.

103   *As it turns out*   Thomas Joiner, *Why People Die by Suicide*
(Cambridge: Harvard University Press, 2005), 193–94.

103   *"Could you tell us"*   Journalistic interview with David Laws,
conducted via Zoom by Angela Gorrell and Joy Moton, September 19, 2019.

104   *Laura Hope was fourteen*   US Drug Enforcement Administration, "Laura Hope Laws, 17, Morphine and Cocaine," August 17,
2018, https://www.getsmartaboutdrugs.gov/consequences/true
-stories/laura-hope-laws-17-morphine-and-cocaine.

104   *Being given prescription opioids*   Richard Miech et al., "Prescription Opioids in Adolescence and Future Opioid Misuse,"
Pediatrics 136, no. 5 (November 2015): e1169–e1177.

104   *Misuse of prescription opioids*   Centers for Disease Control
and Prevention, "Heroin Overdose Data," https://www.cdc.gov
/drugoverdose/data/heroin.html; Laurie Meyers, "Infusing
hope amid despair," September 24, 2013, https://ct.counseling
.org/2018/09/infusing-hope-amid-despair/.

105   *Opiates produce feelings*   The Recovery Village, "Exploring

Why Opiates Make You Feel Good," March 1, 2019, https:// www.therecoveryvillage.com/opiate-addiction/exploring-why -opiates-make-you-feel-good/#gref.

105   *They bind to the areas*   CNN Library, "Opioid Crisis Fast Facts," *CNN*, October 18, 2017, https://www.cnn.com/2017/09/18 /health/opioid-crisis-fast-facts/index.html.

105   *For a time, opioids magically*   Sullivan, "The Poison We Pick."

105   *After watching a movie*   Kate Fagan, "Split Image," ESPN, web page, May 7, 2015, http://www.espn.com/espn/feature/story /_/id/12833146/instagram-account-university-pennsylvania -runner-showed-only-part-story.

105   *Carli Bushoven, Madison's older sister*   Carli's reflections are based on a journalistic email interview with Carli Bushoven conducted by Angela Gorrell and Joy Moton between September 20 and October 10, 2019.

106   *She was offered scholarships*   Johanna Gretschel, "'What Made Maddy Run' Examines the Brief, Intense Life of Madison Holleran," Flotrack website, July 17, 2017, https://www.flotrack.org /articles/5067931-what-made-maddy-run-examines-the-brief -intense-life-of-madison-holleran.

107   *The overall consensus*   Donna Freitas, *The Happiness Effect: How Social Media Is Driving a Generation to Appear Perfect at Any Cost* (New York: Oxford University Press, 2017).

107   *For most of the college students*   Freitas, *The Happiness Effect*, 14. I first discussed the happiness effect in *Always On: Practicing Faith in a New Media Landscape* (Grand Rapids: Baker Academic, 2019), 114.

107   *Freitas also found*   Freitas, *The Happiness Effect*, 71.

107   *College students compare*   Freitas, *The Happiness Effect*, 14.

108   *For many young people*   Ryan McAnnally-Linz said this to me during an in-person conversation. See also Ryan McAnnally-Linz, "An Unrecognizable Glory: Christian Humility in the Age of Authenticity," PhD diss., Yale University, 2016.

108   *Young people are also*   Jordan McKenzie, "Happiness vs Contentment? A Case for a Sociology of the Good Life," *Journal for the Theory of Social Behavior* 46, no. 3 (2015): 264.

108   *"Like a good brand"*   Gorrell, *Always On*, 79.

109   *You are made to believe*   McKenzie, "Happiness vs Contentment?," 262.

109   *Lynn, forty years old*   In-person journalistic interview with Lynn Harper, in Angela Gorrell's office at Truett Seminary, conducted by Gorrell and Joy Moton, September 24, 2019.

114   *"Deaths of despair"*   Anne Case and Angus Deaton, *Deaths of Despair and the Future of Capitalism* (Princeton: Princeton University Press, 2020).

114   *Despair is an awful teacher*   Jennings, "Joy That Gathers."

Chapter Seven

119   *"How does pain fit into a good life?"*   The Life Worth Living team developed a question about the role of suffering in the good life, together, before spring 2019, my third year of teaching Life Worth Living. This is one version of the question.

119   *It will feel as if*   Angela Gorrell, last lecture for Life Worth Living course, Yale University, April 2019.

119   *If I feel anxious*   Miroslav Volf and Matthew Croasmun discuss Life Worth Living's three-part structure (circumstantial, agential, affective) of visions of the good life in *For the Life of the World: Theology That Makes a Difference* (Grand Rapids: Brazos, 2019), 164, 170, 176.

119   *No vision of the true life*   Miroslav Volf and Matthew Croasmun use the term "true life" in *For the Life of the World*, 13–20, 62–64, 76–80, 180–82.

121   *Along the way*   I am indebted to my colleagues at the Yale Center for Faith and Culture for the language related to becoming "more human."

123   *"The love of God and the void of God"*   Wiman, *My Bright Abyss*, 69.

124   *God's primary response*   Michael Petrow shared with me in conversation that "the best answer to theodicy is theophany."

125   *If there is anything*   James Cone, *God of the Oppressed* (Maryknoll, NY: Orbis Books, 1997), 75.

127   *But for a few minutes*   Miroslav Volf and Ryan McAnnally-

Linz, private conversation at the Yale Center for Faith and Culture.

128 *We were instead filled with a bright sorrow* Miroslav Volf, lecture on joy, Association of Youth Ministry Educators, annual meeting 2018. Volf was drawing on something Alexander Schmemann wrote about in his journals. Alexander Schmemann, *The Journals of Father Alexander Schmemann, 1973–1983*, trans. Julianna Schmemann (Crestwood, NY: St. Vladimir's Seminary Press, 2000), 137; see also Justin Crisp, "A Bright Sorrow," in Volf and Crisp, *Joy and Human Flourishing*, vii–xviii.

128 *Because joy is God* Andrew Root develops this idea of joy in his book *The End of Youth Ministry? Why Parents Don't Really Care about Youth Groups and What Youth Workers Should Do about It* (Grand Rapids: Baker Academic, 2020). See particularly chaps. 9, 11, and 12.

128 *"The present experience of God's being"* Root, *The End of Youth Ministry?*, chaps. 9, 11, and 12.

Chapter Eight

137 *Perhaps it was our version* After a member of a Jewish family dies, family members sit on short stools, which symbolizes the person being "brought low," and they mourn in a number of ways. See "Sitting Shiva," web page, https://www.shiva.com/learning-center/sitting-shiva/.

138 *Joy is a counteragent* Oriana R. Aragón, "'Tears of Joy' and 'Tears and Joy?': Personal Accounts of Dimorphous and Mixed Expressions of Emotion," *Motivation and Emotion* 41, no. 3 (2017): 370–92.

139 *Joy is not dependent* Miroslav Volf, lecture on joy, Association of Youth Ministry Educators, annual meeting 2018.

140 *Joy is excess* Mathewes, "Toward a Theology of Joy," 66.

140 *"Often accompanies a realization"* Nel Noddings, "Enhancing the Ideal: Joy," in *Caring: A Relational Approach to Ethics and Moral Education* (Berkeley: University of California Press, 2013), 132.

140 *Anguish often follows* George Vaillant, *Spiritual Evolution:*

How We Are Wired for Faith, Hope, and Love (New York: Broadway Books, 2008), 124. See also Philip C. Watkins, "Appraising Joy," *Journal of Positive Psychology* 15, no. 1 (2020): 25–29. DOI: 10.1080/17439760.2019.1685570.

140 *"Music, the birth of a baby"* N. T. Wright, *The Millennium Myth: Hope for a Postmodern World* (Louisville: Westminster John Knox, 1999), 39–40.

140 *I've learned that* Noddings, "Enhancing the Ideal: Joy," 132.

141 *Joy is an illumination* The Polish poet Adam Zagajewski distinguishes joy from happiness by explaining that happiness is a political condition and joy an illumination. Adam Potkay, *The Story of Joy* (New York: Cambridge University Press, 2007), 22.

141 *Nina's idea was* Center for Council website, https://www.cen terforcouncil.org/.

141 *"Age-old practice"* Center for Council, "What Is Council?," web page, https://www.centerforcouncil.org/what-is-council .html.

141 *Ultimately, they agreed* Phone conversation between Nina Lau-Branson and Angela Gorrell, September 2019.

143 *Like Nina's groups* Mary Clark Moshella, "Elements of Joy in Lived Practices of Care," in Volf and Crisp, *Joy and Human Flourishing*, 106–7.

143 *Together, as Nina's Council circles do* Rick Hanson, "Seven Facts about the Brain That Incline the Mind to Joy," in *Measuring the Immeasurable: The Scientific Case for Spirituality* (Boulder, CO: Sounds True, 2008), 278–79.

144 *Human beings, young and old* Joiner, *Why People Die by Suicide*, 96–97.

144 *Like Nina's Council circles, we need to pick up* Laurie Meyers, "Infusing Hope amid Despair," *Counseling Today*, web page, September 24, 2018, https://ct.counseling.org/2018/09/infusing -hope-amid-despair/.

145 *"Memory within a particular, cultural group"* Almeda Wright and Anne Wimberly, "Memory and Joy," lecture for the Youth Ministry Institute, Yale Center for Faith and Culture, May 3, 2017. For the basic ideas they give in this lecture, see the brief video at https://www.youtube.com/watch?v=8hOO96TzVR4.

145 *"To be a part of this cultural memory"* Almeda Wright and Anne Wimberly, "Memory and Joy."

147 *"A Christian community"* Henri Nouwen, *The Wounded Healer: Ministry in Contemporary Society* (New York: Doubleday Image Book, 1979), 94.

147 *She always helped me* Mark Lau Branson, "Disruptions Meet Practical Theology," web page, https://fullerstudio.fuller.edu /disruptions-meet-practical-theology/.

148 *"If empathy is what can erase shame"* Brené Brown has spoken widely about shame and the power of empathy. "Shame Is Lethal," *SuperSoul Sunday*, Oprah Winfrey Network, https:// www.youtube.com/watch?v=GEBjNv5M784.

148 *"When we become aware"* Nouwen, *The Wounded Healer*, 93.

148 *"Wounds into wisdom"* Treasure Ramirez, testimonial, Baylor New Faculty Orientation, August 19, 2019.

149 *"Despair seems to"* James H. Cone, *The Cross and the Lynching Tree* (Maryknoll, NY: Orbis Books, 2013), 14.

149 *"Casts a positive vision"* Crisp, "A Bright Sorrow," xvii.

149 *Whereas apathy is a result* Matthew Kuan Johnson, "Joy: A Review of the Literature and Suggestions for Future Directions," *Journal of Positive Psychology* 15, no. 1 (2020): 5–24. DOI: 10.1080/17439760.2019.1685581. Johnson's article for the *Journal of Positive Psychology* discusses Aquinas's point about acedia being the opposite of joy and calls for further research and scholarship about joy and acedia. See also Thomas Aquinas, *Summa Theologiae* II-II.35.1.

149 *We need a way of life* Andrew Sullivan, "America's New Religions," *Intelligencer*, December 7, 2018, http://nymag .com/intelligencer/2018/12/andrew-sullivan-americas-new -religions.html.

149 *During the course of* Matthew Croasmun, "What's Worth Wanting," lecture for Grace Farms, December 10, 2019.

149 *"The striving and struggling"* Frankl, *Man's Search for Meaning*, 127.

150 *In other words, there are many ways* Noddings, "Enhancing the Ideal: Joy," 137.

151 *"The vegetarian who now dislikes"* Herdt, "Why the Pursuit

of Happiness Is a Bad Idea," April 2, 2018, Yale "Seek Well" Initiative, 4–5. Emphasis added to the final quotation.

151 *We do not often* Steve Reis, "The Sixteen Strivings for God," *Zygon* 39, no. 2 (June 2004): 306.

151 *When you feel* Noddings, "Enhancing the Ideal: Joy," 132.

152 *Amy rejoiced over* Warren Kinghorn, "Love's Rest: Thomas Aquinas and the Psychology of Joy," prepared for Yale Center for Faith & Culture consultation on "Joy, Human Nature and Human Destiny," September 12–13, 2014, 5.

165 *And it meant, in light of* Cone, *God of the Oppressed*, 112.

166 *Michelle is more familiar with joy* Sarah A. Schnitker, Juliette L. Ratchford, and Rosemond T. Lorona, "How Can Joy Escape Jingle-Jangle? Virtue and Telos Conceptualizations as Alternative Approaches to the Scientific Study of Joy," *Journal of Positive Psychology* 15, no. 1 (October 2019): 44–48.

166 *She is finding value* David Kenneth Pooler, Terry Wolfer, and Miriam Freeman, "Finding Joy in Social Work II: Intrapersonal Sources," *Social Work* 59, no. 3 (July 2014): 213–21.

Chapter Nine

169 *We cannot put joy* Carroll E. Izard *Patterns of Emotions: A New Analysis of Anxiety and Depression* (New York: Academic Press, 1972), 564. Joy cannot be produced voluntarily.

169 *We can be ready* Karl Barth, *Church Dogmatics*, III/4, *The Doctrine of Creation* (Edinburgh: T&T Clark, 1961), 378–79.

169 *We can do things* Mathewes describes joy as "a reality best understood in the 'middle voice,'" in "Toward a Theology of Joy," 66.

170 *So in addition* Noddings, "Enhancing the Ideal: Joy," 146. See also Barth, *Church Dogmatics*, III/4, 378.

170 *Johnny responded to* "Johnny Knoxville Opens Up about Life as a Dad & Staging Intervention for Steve-O," *Access*, October 20, 2010, https://www.accessonline.com/articles/johnny -knoxville-opens-up-about-life-as-a-dad-staging-intervention -for-steve-o-91817.

172 *"Appropriately disturbed"* Thompson describes this as *joy notwithstanding*, joy that looks "forward in hope anticipating

the action of God to remove all affliction and tribulation," in "Reflections on Joy in the Bible," 37.

172   *The call to joy*   Crisp, "A Bright Sorrow," viii.

172   *"Feelings have to be mentionable"*   Fred Rogers in *Won't You Be My Neighbor?*, documentary directed by Morgan Neville, produced by Morgan Neville, Caryn Capotosto, and Nicholas Ma, October 18, 2019.

172   *"All of us have invisible"*   Kathy Reid, sermon at Truett Theological Seminary chapel, October 8, 2019.

172   *More of us need invisible neon signs*   Alison Cook and Kimberly Miller, *Boundaries for Your Soul: How to Turn Your Overwhelming Thoughts and Feelings into Your Greatest Allies* (Nashville: Nelson Books, 2018).

172   *Befriending emotions starts*   Alison Cook and Kimberly Miller, "How to Turn Your Overwhelming Thoughts and Feelings into Your Greatest Allies," web page, June 28, 2018, https://www.faithgateway.com/turn-overwhelming-thoughts-feelings-greatest-allies/#.XZevFC2ZOqA.

173   *Like other powerful emotions*   Brené Brown and Oprah Winfrey, "Joy: It's Terrifying," *SuperSoul Sunday*, Oprah Winfrey Network, https://www.youtube.com/watch?v=RKVoBWSPfOw.

173   *The moment we experience joy*   Brené Brown and Oprah Winfrey, "Joy: It's Terrifying."

173   *Not only do we need*   David Steere, "Our Capacity for Sadness and Joy: An Essay on Life before Death," in *Theology of Joy*, ed. Johann Baptist Metz and Jean-Pierre Jossua (New York: Herder and Herder, 1974), 15–16.

173   *And we need this permission*   Steere, "Our Capacity for Sadness and Joy," 15–16.

174   *Some people have a joyful disposition*   Michael F. Scheier and Charles S. Carver, "On the Power of Positive Thinking: The Benefits of Being Optimistic," *Current Directions in Psychological Science* 2, no. 1 (1993): 26–30, https://doi.org/10.1111/1467-8721.ep10770572. See also Miroslav Volf, "Miroslav Volf Delves into the Theology of Joy: A Q&A," May 21, 2018, https://religionnews.com/2018/05/21/miroslav-volf-delves-into-the-theology-of-joy-a-qa/?mc_cid=dced8b263f&mc_eid=ef4d6f8c5a.

175   *"Calls to rejoice"*   Thompson, "Reflections on Joy in the Bible,"
34. Emphasis added.

175   *"Joy is characterized"*   Kinghorn, "Love's Rest," 2. Emphasis
added.

175   *"Joy is best experienced"*   Miroslav Volf, "The Crown of the
Good Life: A Hypothesis," in Volf and Crisp, *Joy and Human
Flourishing*, 132–33.

176   *Unfortunately, experiences of intense joy*   Peter H. Van Ness,
"Endangered Bliss: Reflections on Joy and Religion," *Journal of
Religion and Health* 35, no. 3 (Fall 1996): 223.

176   *"Convey the impression"*   Rowan Williams, *Being Disciples: Es-
sentials of the Christian Life* (Grand Rapids: Eerdmans, 2016),
86.

176   *"The tonality of Christianity"*   Schmemann, *Journals*, 137.

176   *Instead, during sports events*   Brené Brown, "Why Experiencing
Joy and Pain in a Group Is So Powerful," *Greater Good Magazine*,
January 19, 2019, https://greatergood.berkeley.edu/article/item
/why_experiencing_joy_and_pain_in_a_group_is_so_powerful.

176   *"They are so deeply"*   Brown, "Why Experiencing Joy and Pain
in a Group Is So Powerful."

177   *It makes sense because*   Kayla Molnar, "Exploring Connections
between College Students' Purpose and Deliberate Outdoor
Adventure Activities," ProQuest Dissertations Publishing, 2017.
Web, 81–83.

177   *Being in creation*   Molnar, "Outdoor Adventure Activities,"
81–83.

177   *Outdoor activities give*   Molnar, "Outdoor Adventure Activities," 66–80.

178   *Suddenly, mundane practices*   Barth, *Church Dogmatics*, III/4,
381. Barth discusses joy in nature as well as joy in the midst of
everyday work.

178   *Kayaking and mussel collecting*   Joiner, *Why People Die by
Suicide*, 317.

179   *There is a physical nature*   N. T. Wright, "Joy: New Testament
Perspectives and Questions," in Volf and Crisp, *Joy and Human
Flourishing*, 42.

181   *Joy often follows gratitude*   Watkins and Emmons et al., "Joy

Is a Distinct Positive Emotion: Assessment of Joy and Relationship to Gratitude and Well-being," *The Journal of Positive Psychology* 13, no. 5 (2018): 522–39.

181   *"What seems to compromise"*   Tomas Sedlacek, "Economic and Theological Impossibility of Joy," prepared for Yale Center for Faith & Culture consultation on "State of Joy," September 5–6, 2014, 5.

181   *"Gratitude for what life really is"*   Barth, *Church Dogmatics*, III/4, 378.

183   *"Built to* look for *the bad"*   Hanson, "Seven Facts about the Brain," 276.

183   *This is obviously important*   Hanson, "Seven Facts about the Brain," 277.

183   *"We can close ourselves"*   Barth, *Church Dogmatics*, III/4, 378.

185   *Such is the gift*   Wright and Wimberly, "Memory and Joy." See also Wright, "Joy: New Testament Perspectives and Questions," 43.

189   *"Stories of joy begin"*   Potkay, *The Story of Joy*, 10.

192   *"Already we enjoy"*   Peter Leithart, "What Is Thanks? Daily Eucharist," *Leithart* blog on Patheos, September 14, 2017, https://www.patheos.com/blogs/leithart/2017/09/thanks-daily-eucharist/.

192   *There is a joy*   Thompson, "Reflections on Joy in the Bible," 33.

192   *Perhaps futuristic joy*   Hans Urs von Balthasar discusses joy and suffering in view of the cross and highlights joy as an effect of life and love in *Theo-Drama: Theological Dramatic Theory*, vol. 5, *The Last Act*, trans. Graham Harrison (San Francisco: Ignatius, 1998), 250–56.

195   *On this Wednesday night*   Christine D. Pohl, *Living into Community: Cultivating Practices That Sustain Us* (Grand Rapids: Eerdmans, 2012).

196   *We were trying to express*   Kate Bowler and Jerome Adams, "Jerome Adams: We Belong to Each Other," podcast interview, https://katebowler.com/podcasts/jerome-adams-we-belong-to-each-other/.

196   *"Don't have to do anything sensational"*   Fred Rogers, captured in *Won't You Be My Neighbor?*

197   *"Amazing grace, how sweet the sound"*   "Amazing Grace" was
       published in 1779, with words written in 1772 by John Newton.

Epilogue

203   *Promoting suicide hotlines*   Joiner, *Why People Die by Suicide.*
204   *"Once a person has been saved after a near overdose"*   R. D.
       Weiss et al., "Long-Term Outcomes from the National Drug
       Abuse Treatment Clinical Trials Network Prescription Opioid
       Addiction Treatment Study," *NCBI*, March 6, 2015, https://www
       .ncbi.nlm.nih.gov/pubmed/25818060; Macy, *Dopesick*, 144.
206   *Overdose rates are dramatically rising*   Krystina Murray, "The
       Tinge of the Drug Crisis: Black Americans and Opioids," Ad-
       diction Center website, accessed September 11, 2018, https://
       www.addictioncenter.com/community/the-tinge-of-the-drug
       -crisis-black-americans-and-opioids/; Peter Jamison and Whit-
       ney Shefte, "Falling Out: A Generation of African American
       Heroin Users Is Dying in the Opioid Epidemic Nobody Talks
       About," *The Washington Post*, December 18, 2018, https://www
       .washingtonpost.com/graphics/2018/local/opioid-epidemic
       -and-its-effect-on-african-americans/.
207   *"Fentanyl is poised"*   David Armstrong, "Dope Sick," *Stat News*,
       August 2, 2016, https://www.statnews.com/feature/opioid
       -crisis/dope-sick/. Emphasis added.
207   *While white Americans use opioids*   Clairmont Griffith, Ber-
       nice La France, Clayton Bacchus, and Gezzer Ortega, "The
       Effects of Opioid Addiction on the Black Community," *Inter-
       national Journal of Collaborative Research on Internal Med-
       icine & Public Health*, http://internalmedicine.imedpub.com
       /the-effects-of-opioid-addiction-on-the-black-community
       .php?aid=23302; Orla Kennedy, "The Opioid Crisis in Black
       Communities: Who Is Paying Attention?," *Community Cata-
       lyst*, accessed February 20, 2019, https://www.communitycat
       alyst.org/blog/the-opioid-crisis-in-black-communities-who-is
       -paying-attention#.XYts2C2ZNos; Keturah James and Ayana
       Jordan, "The Opioid Crisis in Black Communities," *SAGE Jour-*

nals, July 17, 2018, https://journals.sagepub.com/doi/abs/10 .1177/1073110518782949?journalCode=lmec.

207   *However, heroin has been destructive*   Murray, "The Tinge of the Drug Crisis."

207   *The response to crack cocaine*   Drug Policy Alliance, "10 Facts about Cocaine," web page, August 2018, http://www.drugpolicy .org/drug-facts/cocaine-and-crack-facts.

208   *Among illicit drugs*   Austin Frakt, "Overshadowed by the Opioid Crisis: A Comeback by Cocaine," *The New York Times,* March 5, 2018, https://www.nytimes.com/2018/03/05/upshot /overshadowed-by-the-opioid-crisis-a-comeback-by-cocaine .html.

208   *Boys who grow up*   Adam Looney and Nicholas Turner, "Work and Opportunity before and after Incarceration," Brookings Institution website, March 14, 2018, https://www.brookings .edu/research/work-and-opportunity-before-and-after -incarceration/.

208   *And while Black and white Americans*   NAACP, "Criminal Justice Factsheet," web page, https://www.naacp.org/criminal -justice-fact-sheet/.